M000169899

Keepin' On

Living Well with Parkinson's Disease

Keepin' On

Living Well with Parkinson's Disease

Robert J. Silver

KEEPIN' ON: LIVING WELL WITH PARKINSON'S DISEASE
Copyright © 2018 by Robert J. Silver
All rights reserved.

Printed in the United States of America.

No part of this book may be used or reproduced in any
manner whatsoever without written permission, except in
the case of brief quotations contained in critical articles
or reviews. For more information, contact Nighthawk Press
at nighthawkpress.com.

ISBN: 978-0-9986807-2-9
Library of Congress Control Number: 2017918565

Front cover photo: Dianne Frost
Back cover photo: Steve Fox
Cover and interior page design: Lesley Cox,
FEEL Design Associates, Taos, New Mexico
feeldesignassociates.com

Editing: Steven Fox, Ph.D., and Barbara L. Scott,
Final Eyes, Taos, New Mexico, finaleyes.net

Type is set in PT Serif

NIGHTHAWK PRESS
TAOS, NEW MEXICO

For Dianne Frost ... my wife ... my life.

*In memory of Larry Schreiber, M.D. (1947-2016) —
husband, father, grandfather, physician, humanitarian,
adventurer, and inspiration to many — all profits from the sales
of* Keepin' On: Living Well with Parkinson's Disease *will go
to Parkinson's disease research, education, and support.*

Contents

Prologue

How am I moving? Medicine kicked in? Will it last through this reception, wedding, funeral, party, dinner, tennis lesson, round of golf, plane ride, concert, conversation? How much longer until I can eat something and not interfere with the medicine's uptake? When is the next dose?

Parkinson's, this chronic, progressive, degenerative disease, is always with me. There is no cure. At least not yet. It compromises my balance; makes my movement slow, clumsy, and uncoordinated; and periodically causes my legs to freeze up, imprisoning me in my own body. But its most pernicious aspect is its intrusion into my thoughts. With each movement, it commandeers my consciousness and triggers endless rumination. Though drug therapies may moderate my motor symptoms to a point and for a time, there's no medication to block Parkinson's invasion of my mind.

Along with the million diagnosed Americans living with Parkinson's disease, I'm mired in the fight of my life for the quality of my life. But I don't want people to feel sorry for me. I have no use for sympathy or pity. In my age cohort, everybody has something. Some struggle with life-threatening conditions. Mine is not one of them. I'm more likely to die *with* Parkinson's than *from* it. It's more a constant pain in the ass, forcing itself upon me, distorting and coloring my every move. I should say every *intended* move, since I can't reliably make my body do what I wish it to do. It's like a recalcitrant child, dragging its feet in opposition to a parental demand.

Now well into my 70s, living a life that I choose — as opposed to one that has been pressed on me — is a continuing challenge. When first diagnosed with Parkinson's, I believed I was facing a life that might not be worth living. But more than a dozen years later, I'm far more active than many my age who don't have a movement disorder.

Many Parkinson's patients live more limited lives than mine. I'm one of the fortunate ones. My doctor is an acclaimed neurologist who specializes in treating this disease. The pharmaceuticals in her bag of tricks control my symptoms surprisingly well without unacceptable side effects. I'm also blessed that my caregiving wife energetically assumes the roles of virtual personal trainer, bar-setting exercise partner, and eagle-eyed sentinel, ever vigilant for promising treatment developments. Finally, there is my deeply ingrained inclination never to give in or give up.

Since it's impossible to write about a subject without devoting thought to it, I was initially apprehensive at the prospect of writing about Parkinson's. It had already colonized much of the landscape of my mind. Granting the disease additional cerebral territory seemed like inviting it to occupy and oppress still more of my thinking. But a serendipitous encounter with a fellow Parkinson's patient persuaded me that I had to write about it. Overall, this chance mountain meeting's impact on my thinking and behavior was so life-altering that it deserves elaboration. This additional detail is offered in a subsequent chapter ("A Surprise Encounter"). Absent this chance event, *Keepin' On* might not have existed.

Ultimately, *Keepin' On: Living Well with Parkinson's Disease* recounts the binds, grinds, disappointments, and occasional triumphs in my struggle with this disease. Written for those who are similarly afflicted and for the people who love and care for us, I hope to help inoculate us against the soul-savaging corrosiveness of hopelessness, despair, and diminished desire. This is my version of the Parkinson's story, the details of which may vary much from one person to another yet still share a core inner world of dogged resistance to the disease's assault on body and mind. In the end, it is the chronicle of my personal refusal to surrender my cherished hopes and dreams, offered with the wish that it may encourage my fellow Parkinson's patients to also keep on keepin' on.

A Tale of Two Bodies[1]

As with all mornings, I'm awake far too early. It's between 3 and 5 a.m. I'm in the depths of parkinsonian near paralysis. All movement is protracted, slow-motion effort. My balance and coordination are severely compromised. The most minimal motion demands my total concentration and planning. I'll need a repeated cocktail of medicines just to get through the day.

I inch my way to the edge of our king-size bed. Dianne's soft, rhythmic breathing confirms that she's still asleep. I leave the bedside lamp off so as not to wake her. To find my way, I rely on a night-light's faint glow and on moonlight filtering into our bedroom.

I move my frozen legs beyond the edge of the bed and push myself up to a seated position. My legs hang down toward the tile floor. I feel around for the iPad I'd positioned on the bedside nightstand the previous evening, when I had more control of my body. It's my link to humanity as I await the return of my ability to move. At this moment, I'm like one of those snakes you see on asphalt roadways, warming their bodies and their cold blood so they can move.

Drugs are my asphalt-roadway equivalent. At 5 a.m., I'll begin a temporary, biochemically based cycle. But for now, I must make my medication-free way across the enormous 15-foot distance to our bathroom.

I'm finally standing next to our bed, clutching the iPad to my chest. I reach out into the darkness with my free arm for support of the chair just beyond the nightstand. I shuffle my bare feet from floor tile to floor tile, feeling each successive grout line. Each marks 13 additional inches of progress toward my goal.

At last, I reach the bathroom doorway. Twisting my body through the opening, I feel around for the door handle and then for the vanity counter. I close the door behind me and switch on the bathroom lights.

The clock on the counter reads 4:39 a.m. Still 21 minutes to the 5 a.m. witching hour, when the magic of modern medicine can begin. I'll swallow a handful of pills to get moving. Once the medication reaches its full effect, I'll likely have some two hours of relatively normal movement before I need the next dose. I'll repeat this three-hour medication cycle over the next 15 hours.

In the lighted bathroom, I keep one hand on the vanity counter as I make my way to the toilet and relief. Pocketing the pill case organized the previous evening, I retrace my steps back through our dark bedroom.

I'm bound for our home's central living area, some 20 feet away. Steadying myself with a succession of improvised handholds, I inch my way to and through a doorway to the rest of the house. I'm cautious. I don't want to fall. I swing this door closed behind me and reach for the light switch. I can see again.

It's now 5 a.m. I must recharge my depleted neurotransmitters. I grasp a waiting water glass, open the pill case, and remove two Stalevos, three Requips, an Azilect, and half an Amantadine tablet. I focus my full attention on the pills to make sure I've got the correct combination. I swallow the seven pills in one gulp and reconfirm the time. I'll still have to wait an hour for the medication to kick in.

I can't get much serious work done in this state, so I content myself with reading email and watching the morning news on TV. I'm sleep-deprived and impatient as I wait for the medicine to take effect. I hope I don't need to make another bathroom journey in the interim.

I eye the clock, willing the time to pass and the medicine to work. But time moves excruciatingly slowly. It's now 5:40. The medicine has probably been at work long enough for me to make my way back to Dianne.

I open our bedroom door, move across the dark room, and climb into bed. The clock radio suddenly fills the air with NPR's "Morning Edition." Dianne begins to stir. I edge toward her. We search for a best-fit intertwining of our bodies. I absorb her soft, satisfying warmth pressed against me, shielding her from contact with my cold fingers and toes. My mobility has now returned, but I don't want to budge. I'm content with the deep, restorative pleasure of holding her in my arms.

After about 15 cherished minutes, I must get going. I dare not linger — the medication's effectiveness won't last forever. I bound from our shared bed, now appearing much like a normal person. My gait, balance, and coordination show just slight signs of impairment. Only a trained eye would detect the now-subtle signs of this disease that torments me so.

As the day proceeds, I continue my clock watching — juggling my time, meals, and anticipated activity — sometimes appearing impatient to the uninformed. This is the structure of a life lived in three-hour blocks of chemically dependent time.

I sometimes joke about being a walking chemistry experiment. Nevertheless, I'm damned fortunate that the drugs manage my symptoms well, and that I have the resources to obtain them. They allow me to hike, bike, ski, snowshoe, play tennis, sail, and even dance. Each Parkinson's case is different. Most are not as fortunate as I am.

But it's an odd, if not bizarre, existence, this yo-yoing back and forth between periods of near immobility and times when I look almost normal. Which body I'll inhabit in any given instant is always an open question.

Right now, I'm Clark Kent, donning his Superman costume and changing his identity. I'm nearly hyperactive, moving from place to place rapidly and almost gracefully. Since I can't predict the drugs' effectiveness from one moment to the next, I feel compelled to pack in all that I can before the inevitable crash. At these times, my drive to do it all is so strong that I may be a bit reckless. Dianne sometimes watches with dread as I move from one recreational activity to another, then to some set of deferred household chores, and finally on to some formal exercise. I grab as much life as possible while I can.

The middle hour of each three-hour period is prime time. It's when I'm likely to be at my peak physical ability. Since eating protein within an hour of taking one of my primary medicines will block its effectiveness, this golden middle hour is the one time I can eat whatever I damn well please. Most people don't live their lives on my rigid meal and medicine schedule, so it complicates plans with friends. I try to alter my medication routine, covertly maneuvering around the course of a shared meal, if possible, to prevent this intrusive fact of my life from invading the lives of those around me. Parkinson's so pervades my consciousness that I do all I can to thwart its further encroachment.

Sometimes I kid myself into thinking these periods of more normal balance won't come to a crashing halt. I may even forget a dose. If I do, I'm painfully reminded that potent drugs rule my life. My rude reawakening to this reality is striking. Suddenly, it's back! The paralyzing cloak of symptoms descends.

Even when I do stick to a rigid routine of medication, meals, and activity, sometimes the medication just fails to act as I hope it will. In any instant, I'm uncertain what I'll be able to do and how well I'll be able to do it.

On this day, I'm out alone on the golf course. None of my buddies are available, and I'm not averse to a solitary outing. I'll just hit two balls for each hole, as if I had a companion. It's a bright, sunny day, late in the fall golfing season. The majestic mountains rimming our high-desert valley home shimmer in the area's legendary light. The crisp, cool breeze on my face hints at the coming season. I feel alive, invigorated, and amazed to play this game that requires some balance and coordination. When

I golf with friends who know I have Parkinson's disease, I secretly smile at their surprise when I tee off. I often hit the ball farther and straighter than they would ever have expected.

So, golf bag over my shoulder, I'm walking the course. I've attended to the details of my food and medication schedule. Then, without warning, I feel a vague sense of compromised coordination in my left leg. It's beginning to drag. I must concentrate on it to lift it and move it forward.

Oh, shit! Not now! Not here!

I've still got four holes to go, and my medicine has stopped working. With each step, I remind myself how to walk. Every step is an ordeal. There's nobody around, and I've got to get through the rest of the course.

Surprisingly and for reasons unknown, I'm sometimes able to walk better backward than forward. So, there I am, alone in the middle of this vast open space, carrying my golf clubs, glancing back over my shoulder from time to time, all while walking in reverse.

As I make my way to the clubhouse and to my parked car, frustration and disappointment swallow whole my afternoon joy and exuberance. I have rapidly descended from a pinnacle of pleasure to a depth of despair. Later, over dinner with Dianne, my sense of humor starts to digest and metabolize this day of golf. Though painful in the moment, I will transform it into one of my favored funny stories.

By the end of the day, I've come full circle. I'm emotionally and physically depleted. As I get into bed, I sense the medication wearing off. Without drugs, my mobility will continue to diminish until morning, when the cycle begins again. I use what ability I still possess to arrange my morning pills.

Lights out, I feel around for Dianne. As if in some slapstick comedy, I must first free my arm — the one I've managed to pin beneath the weight of my own body. Gone are the days of a reliable body's graceful overture. As Dianne moves to meet my labored effort, I yearn both for her and for sleep. I'll likely be awake again in some five hours.

As I drift off to sleep, a fierce, unseen war rages within me. With the coming dawn, I wonder, which of the two distinct bodies that vie for dominion will be mine? In any given day, hour, minute, second, I don't know which body will prevail. Will it be the one of paralysis or one of movement? The body of my dreams or the body of my nightmares?

---

1) Earlier versions of this essay were both performed in the Taos Onstage–SOMOS Readers Theater production "You Never Know," April 15, 2015, and posted on The Michael J. Fox Foundation for Parkinson's Research FoxFeed Blog ("Keep On Keepin' On: One Man's Experience with PD"), June 21, 2016.

In a Season of Loss

The whole thing is getting me at least a bit pissed off. Earlier life stages had their transitional struggles, but none as dismal as the one that defines this current time. For us septuagenarians, it's a season of loss. What began as a trickle now evokes the specter of a torrent of diminished connections and possibilities.

First, it's friends and acquaintances deciding that our small mountain town is too isolated, too lacking in state-of-the-art medical services to spend one's last years here. Either independently or bidden by concerned family members, they have been relocating closer to worried loved ones. Consequently, they have been gradually departing my life's orbit.

Then it's valued acquaintances suddenly dropping dead. Though not my nearest and dearest, Charlie and Steve each had an outsized impact on the nature and quality of life in this place that I intend to depart feet first. I treasured my contacts with them, was enriched knowing them, and am diminished by the loss of them.

The losses then hit closer to home. Cindy, a long-time Texas friend, is dead within months of our learning of her cancer diagnosis. Donna, a treasured Taos friend, becomes ill while traveling abroad. She, too, is diagnosed with an aggressive cancer. She enters hospice and dies within days. Jeff, another dear Texas friend, finally succumbs to a months-long downward spiral following a double lung transplant.

This is the natural order of things. But why can't the people I cherish all be defying the odds like my childhood friend Mark? He was still going strong 20 years after a crude, by contemporary standards, heart transplant. But wait! He, too, finally surrendered. And there's Dirk, surviving a "95 percent fatal" dissecting aorta. Has this life become the litany of the dead?

In tandem with this building wave of short-circuited relationships, there are the inevitable losses of ability brought on by aging and/or disease. At this stage, either you contract some bad disease or your friends do. It's a season of making do, struggling to hold onto abilities, fighting for a future of occasional rays of fulfillment that pierce the blanketing fog of diminishing possibilities.

Among those in my age cohort who have not yet faced compelling medical conditions, there is talk of an intimacy invisibility that envelops them. With advancing age, they speak with wistful resignation of earlier sexually charged eras. Bemoaning their relegation to the status of those whose erotic time has passed, they mourn the loss of a prized piece of themselves.

Then, one brisk, sunny fall morning in this season of loss, I'm out alone practicing my tennis serve. Though Parkinson's disease would seem to render playing tennis unlikely, I persist. There are better days when medication supports adequate movement, and there are disappointing ones, when I am relatively immobile.

Since serving does not require me to react as quickly as chasing down an opponent's shot, it offers a unique possibility for gaining competitive advantage. Nothing happens in a tennis match until the ball is served. In this instant alone, I am in control of the point. Though serve placement and pace require timing and coordination, these skills are more manageable for me than the instantaneous reading and reacting essential to other aspects of the game. It's routine for me to practice serving prior to my weekly lesson and mixed-doubles play.

My friend Maureen drives her car into the parking area adjacent to my practice court. Former next-door neighbors, she and her husband and Dianne and I have been friends for a dozen years. Over the months, I have casually noted Maureen's routine. Arriving for her regular physical-therapy appointments at the spa where we are members, she typically seeks a remote, shaded parking space adjacent to my practice court. We usually wave or nod in acknowledgment of one another.

This day brings something different. Maureen alters her routine. Instead of walking toward the spa's entrance, she heads in the opposite direction, straight toward me. She reaches the chain link fence separating us. She's obviously on a mission. Her determined demeanor makes clear she has something to say. I interrupt practice and go over to greet her.

She declares, "While you've been out here taking tennis lessons and practicing, you've also been teaching the rest of us. Watching you week after week, we've been learning from you. You've been showing us how to face illnesses that may be in store for us. You've taught us about courage. I've wanted to tell you that."

Startled and a bit embarrassed, I demur. "Well, I can be pretty determined," I respond.

"You've demonstrated great courage," insists this spouse of a retired U.S. Marine Corps colonel.

I'm at an uncharacteristic loss for words. Though flattering, her depiction is well beyond the universe of language that I would apply to myself. I manage to mumble my thanks to her for sharing this with me. With that, she raises her hand to the chain link fence between us. I reflexively mirror her movement. Our hands make contact in a void in the fence's steel mesh. She has not merely touched my hand. She has touched my heart.

Within this season of loss, there is this unexpected find. It's something beyond me and worth cherishing. I gain added strength from the knowledge that others may be watching me, rooting for me, counting on me, feeling encouraged by me. These unseen observers solidify my resolve. They add a cause beyond my own, one that obliges me to keep faith with any who might find inspiration in my actions. How could I not persist when they may be comforted by my effort? I carry on, then, for them and for me. I'm unexpectedly reinvigorated as I return to tennis and resume my journey, seeking a path amid losses that will surely lie ahead.

A Surprise Encounter

Parkinson's disease is far down the list of subjects to which I ever intended to devote additional attention. It's a disease already so intrusive that it occupies much too much of my consciousness. My ongoing struggle has been focused on thinking about it as little as possible. Fat chance! Yet a serendipitous encounter in an unlikely place changed all that.

A Father's Day hike to Taos Ski Valley's 10,800-foot-elevation Williams Lake had become a tradition for our friends, Susan and Rollie, and their dog, Schatzie. They have been good friends of ours for several years. Dianne and I have traveled with them, sailed with them, and been guests in each other's homes. Along with our dog, Shadow, we readily accepted their invitation to join them on this glorious day hike.

While stamina is not a particular problem for me, hiking is always uncertain. But Susan and Rollie are close friends who would understand my potential balance and coordination glitches. Together, we have endured any number of travel mishaps. I was confident that they could generously roll with whatever transpired.

On this day, as we start up the trail, it soon becomes clear that at least for the time being the going for me will be halting and hesitant. I will literally have trouble walking and chewing gum at the same time. Dianne and Susan and the dogs are already up ahead. As if he had not already noticed, I explain my current situation to Rollie.

"I can either walk or talk right now. I can't do both. So, we can stop and talk or I can walk without talking."

Rollie is a wonderful conversationalist and is at ease carrying the full communication load for us. I focus my attention on each foot placement over the rooted and rocky trail. He intuitively adjusts his pace to mine. Determined to proceed with the climb, I hope my medicine will kick in soon.

At this point, the hike to the lake is a protracted slog for me. The wide, rocky path that begins our journey is not my favorite part of the hike, except in winter when it is deep in snow and traversed on snowshoes.

We pause for a pit stop and a brief conversational opportunity. While struggling up the trail, I've been silently contemplating seeking the temporary refuge of humor to assuage my increasing discomfort at holding the group to this snail's pace. In an obviously absurd vein, I begin spouting some drivel about how different everything will be when I'm running things.

Rollie may well see right through my transparent ploy. Nevertheless, he obligingly chuckles in acknowledgment of my attempt to inject humor into a thus far less-than-stellar hiking experience.

We are finally into the more heavily forested section of the trail. Given the near-perfect holiday-weekend weather, it will soon become more crowded than we have ever seen it. Taos is a small town, and we repeatedly encounter friends, acquaintances, and even genial strangers as we erratically continue our climb.

My painfully slow pace toward our destination generates multiple occasions for Susan to check on my status.

"Should we keep going? Do you need to rest? Should we turn back?"

I reassure her, "I'm not in any pain. I'm just slow and clumsy. Let's keep going. Sorry to slow things down so much."

Dianne has been through this scenario many times. She knows the drill. Just let me find my pace and rhythm, and hope that the pharmaceuticals soon become active.

By the time we reach Williams Lake, my medicine is finally working. I can now actually enjoy the lake and its environs. We linger a bit prior to beginning our descent, taking in the beauty and majesty of the mountain peaks that surround us.

Making my way back down the mountain trail, I am now moving well. My body is at last functioning near normal. It induces a temporary high in me; I am near euphoric. To Dianne's consternation, I am virtually jogging down the path back toward the trailhead.

Since it's Father's Day, we've decided to head for a celebratory brunch at a restaurant near the trail's staging area and just beyond the base of one of Taos Ski Valley's chairlifts. Arriving at the restaurant, we find that we are not alone in our judgment that this would be a great place to end a hike.

It's pretty much the only game on this part of the mountain, so we wait our turn to be seated on the sprawling outdoor deck. Eventually, we're directed to an available table and we place our orders. At about that time, a couple we'd earlier encountered on the trail approach the restaurant's deck. Johnny and Kathleen are from Alexandria, Louisiana. They have a vacation home in Angel Fire, about an hour's drive from Taos. They come up the stairs to the deck and are seated next to us.

My companions are absorbed in their conversation and take no particular notice of the new arrivals. My personal radar, however, has sprung into high alert. I am locked onto a target. Though the signs are subtle and Johnny has in fact been engaged in this unlikely hiking activity, I cannot take my eyes off him. I'm almost certain that he, too, has Parkinson's disease. It is said that animals instinctively recognize their own kind. So it may be with those who have Parkinson's disease. I'd bet big money that he's a member of my pack.

Serendipitously, Johnny and Kathleen are seated immediately adjacent to our table. He heads for the restroom, and I turn to his temporarily unaccompanied partner.

"I don't mean to be intrusive, but does your husband happen to belong to my club?"

She hesitates briefly then answers, "You mean Parkinson's? Yes, John has Parkinson's disease."

By the time Johnny returns from the restroom, Kathleen has filled us in on his medical history. He is quickly brought up to speed on the conversation that took place in his absence.

We soon discover other commonalities. John is being followed by a Parkinson's specialty group in Houston. I, too, was a patient there prior to my relocation to Taos five years earlier.

He and Kathleen relate their dissatisfaction with John's current care. I volunteer my far greater satisfaction with my care in Albuquerque. Johnny — a former competitive swimmer and a golfer — is committed to remaining as physically active as possible.

I have encountered a kindred spirit, one of my own kind.

Though I generally refrain from offering advice, whether solicited or not, I suggest to Johnny and Kathleen that he would likely receive better care with my Albuquerque neurologist than he is currently getting in Houston.

"I've had far better care from her than from anyone, anywhere," I declare.

I've unexpectedly become invested in assuring that this relative stranger receives the same high-quality care that I feel so thankful to be getting. It's as if I've instantly become an evangelist for my doctor's knowledge, skill, and compassion. I've effectively nominated myself for the role of Johnny's guardian angel.

The whole thing had taken me quite by surprise. Days later, the post-hike encounter continues to preoccupy me. I'm still puzzled at my unsolicited offering of advice. My time as a university professor comes to mind. It was clear to me then that I never learned something better than when I tried to teach it. In the effort to teach, I learned the lesson ever more deeply. Perhaps this was a partial explanation for my impulsive advice to Johnny. Maybe it was some version of the golden rule, and I was trying to give to Johnny the sort of thing that I would hope someone would offer me.

As I've stated elsewhere, this chance meeting with Johnny and Kathleen had evoked my sense of obligation to share my personal Parkinson's management experience and strategy. Many in our tribe are not faring as well as Johnny and me. Perhaps offering my experience could be of help to some of them and to those who love and care for them. As with my teaching experience, if I could be encouraging to others, I might just wind up feeling even more encouraged myself. We'll see.

But for the Kindness of Strangers

Motoring south on New York City's Westside Highway, we are in synchrony with the majestic Hudson River's flow. The broad expanse of water shimmers in the late afternoon's full fall sunshine. This venerable mile-wide river captivates me. I recall a decades-earlier airliner flight path up the Hudson and back into this city of my birth. As I drive, I gaze nostalgically at the river, as much as safety and prudence allow.

Dianne and I have spent the earlier part of the day visiting with a group of my childhood friends. Now bound for a West 44th Street rental-car return, we are contentedly en route to lower Manhattan. We progress in tandem with the Hudson's inexorable journey to the sea. I drive in silence, while Dianne naps lightly in the passenger seat.

Nearing our destination, the smooth flow of vehicles abruptly changes. We are suddenly mired in Manhattan's legendary traffic, now sprung full-blown into being. The earlier surge of cars, now barely a trickle, holds us captive. We creep along, eying the clock, hoping to avoid exorbitant late-arrival rental-car charges.

Trapped in the stop-and-go traffic, I feel a disappointing though familiar sensation in my left foot. Its tingling numbness presages the failure of my medicine. I know that with the collapse of the medication's effectiveness, my ability to walk will soon be compromised.

I'm not due for another dose of medicine for a couple of hours. I dare not do this sooner for fear of complicating consequences. I anxiously anticipate having to muddle through, yearning for the relief of what in lighter moments I refer to as to as my performance-enhancing drugs.

As we inch toward our immediate destination, I am preoccupied by the prospect of diminished physical mobility. In my distracted state, I misinterpret the area's one-way-street pattern and make a wrong turn. My mistake takes us several blocks out of our way, prolonging our immersion in the jammed traffic.

Finally back on course, we spot the rental-agency sign ahead and slowly maneuver the car into the crowded garage. We must now extricate ourselves and our belongings from the car, deal with the attendant, and make our way to a public-transportation link to our rented apartment.

Damn! Awful timing. Get the luggage out of the trunk. Briefcase, small roll-aboard. Grab Dianne's bag. Has the attendant noticed my odd movements? Dianne's probably disappointed, frustrated. Just need to make it a couple of blocks. Southbound bus, then another block or so to the apartment. Got to phone Jacob about check-in. Restroom stop before leaving the garage. Damn, toilets at the far end of the garage.

Car finally checked in and luggage temporarily deposited beside it, Dianne makes her way to the restroom. Then, it's my turn. My steps are excruciatingly slow, halting, unsteady. At last, I'm through the door and into the barely functional facility. No awards are earned for urban design or cleanliness here. Given the absence of options, it will do.

Dianne is waiting as I emerge. She is unfamiliar with Manhattan and depends on me to lead the way. I'm uncommunicative as I struggle to put one foot in front of the other. It takes all the effort I can muster just to move. I'm focused on moving my legs and maintaining my balance.

"Which way do we go?" Dianne inquires.

"About a block over and one down," I reply, while willing my unresponsive legs to get going.

"Have you called Jacob?" Dianne asks, referring to the apartment rental agent.

"I'll call him now, before we head out," I reply, searching in my coat pocket for my phone.

Call's not going through. Thick concrete garage walls. Text him. Hope he gets it.

"I texted him. Let's go," I announce, as we make our way to the sidewalk at the garage's entrance. "Up the street. We cross at the corner."

My progress is becoming more labored. My legs feel like immovable concrete appendages. Shuffling across a minimally trafficked side street is one thing, but we will soon reach the intersection of 42nd Street and 9th Avenue. It's hard to imagine a more difficult location. Clogged with cars, trucks, buses and pedestrians, there probably couldn't be a worse setting for me to become immobilized. The sprawling 42nd Street crossing feels like it rivals the distance to the Hudson River's far Jersey shore.

Yesterday, my small rolling suitcase glided across La Guardia Airport's crowded concourses. It has now met its match in the assortment of fissures and fractures in the city's aged sidewalks. The small suitcase seems to have an uncanny knack for finding and binding in every crevice along our meandering route. It's difficult to determine whether the bag's wheels are easing or intensifying my load.

Dianne has adjusted her pace to match mine. She mirrors each of my leaden steps. Prior experience has made it clear that I am most at ease without her efforts to intervene. Frustrating though this may be, she waits for me to ask her for help. I'm intent on the challenge of making my limbs obey my wishes. I offer her no immediate guidance.

Overdressed for the Indian summer's temperature, I'm perspiring profusely. I struggle to proceed amid the swirling scrum of humanity. The number and press of motor vehicles and pedestrians seem to rise with every few yards of progress.

Finally, we reach a 9th Avenue southbound bus stop. Dianne has located a ticket kiosk. But we lack either exact change or a required Metro Card. The bus option evaporates.

We have two remaining possibilities: walk the dozen or so blocks to the apartment or hail a taxi. Given my current state of mobility, walking the distance is a nonstarter. The taxi it is.

For the uninitiated, flagging down a cab would seem simple enough. Though eminently appealing, it's a complicated process, now that it's prime taxi-competition time in Midtown Manhattan. Getting a taxi in rush hour will require a set of urban survival skills that I no longer possess and Dianne never acquired. To succeed, you must be vigilant in spotting one of the few available cabs in the stream of traffic, be nimble in attracting the driver's attention, and be assertive in competing with other would-be riders. The absence of even one of these components can doom a prospective passenger's quest.

So here we are at one of the most daunting inter-

sections in the Western world — me, almost immobilized, and Dianne, at least a bit overwhelmed. My
frustration with my halting movement is approaching its zenith. Given Dianne's superior mobility, she
will have to hail the taxi.

"The bus is not going to work," I announce. "We'll
either have to walk or you'll have to hail a cab."

"How do I do that?" she asks.

"We'll have to get over to the other side of the
intersection," I reply, gesturing diagonally to a spot
where we will be more likely to attract an available
taxi. But my effort to explain seems only to confuse
Dianne.

A bystander has noticed our burgeoning bewil-
derment and ineptness. I had glimpsed a fortyish
African-American woman sitting on a low masonry
wall, eating a slice of pizza and chatting with a man
of roughly the same age. She had been casually ob-
serving and evaluating our situation.

She calls out to us, "Where you trying to get to?"

Dianne replies with the address of the rental
apartment.

"You need a taxi," she declares. Nodding in my
direction, she observes, "He ain't walking to no 8th
Avenue and 28th Street. You're never gettin' a taxi
on your own. I'm gonna get you one."

She adds, "My name's Yvonne. I don't want
nothin' from you. I don't want your money. I don't

want nothin'. He can take all the time he needs," she adds, gesturing in my direction.

With that, we are in Yvonne's care. Her New Yorker's eye has sized up the intersection's swirl of people and flow of taxi traffic. "We've got to get over there," she asserts, pointing diagonally across the intersection. This will require crossing two major traffic-clogged streets: first 9th Avenue and then 42nd Street. The prospect of navigating these two traffic arteries is daunting. Digital timers halt the flow of onrushing traffic for 20 seconds. It's more than sufficient time for an average pedestrian, but it's unlikely to be enough time for me.

To focus my attention on safely putting one foot in front of the other and not being distracted by Dianne's and Yvonne's progress, I tell them, "You head across and I'll follow."

They seem ambivalent about leaving me. But they are caught up in the challenge of safely negotiating the crossings. I've left them with little alternative but to proceed.

They make their way across 9th Avenue, as I labor to launch myself into the momentarily navigable intersection. The timer reaches zero and I have merely managed to step off the curb into the street. I will myself back onto the sidewalk, waiting for the timing device to recycle.

Through the crowd, I can now see Dianne and

Yvonne on the opposite side of 9th Avenue. Preparing to make their way across 42nd Street, they repeatedly glance back in my direction, powerless to assist me. Like a runner in starting blocks, I am preparing myself for release into the challenge that I will immediately face. My attention is fixed on the crossing timer's countdown cycle. It flashes 20, and I launch myself into the pack of pedestrians who step as one into the intersection crosswalk.

I am like slow-moving flotsam carried in a faster-flowing stream. Pedestrians glide past the eddy formed in the flow by my sluggish pace. The timer is almost at zero, and I've yet to reach the relative safety of the far shore's sidewalk. Within yards of my curbside destination, I become almost motionless. Traffic will soon be bearing down on me. A young woman steps into the street in my direction, distress and concern writ large on her face.

"Let me help you," she says, reaching simultaneously for my arm and my luggage. She deftly and mercifully extracts me from the approaching vehicles.

"Thanks so much," I tell her, as she hurriedly melts back into the anonymity of the crowd.

I'm now faced with the prospect of the 42nd Street crossing. Dianne and Yvonne are across the intersection waiting for me. Once again, the timer signals my next uncertain foray. Once again, I arrive some yards short of the safety of my sidewalk destination as the timer reaches zero.

A bus is inching toward me as I furiously struggle the final few yards. I'm at the mercy of the driver's skill, patience, and judgment as I slowly shuffle forward over the remaining bit of ground toward safety. A man reaches out of the crowd for me, guiding me and assuring my safe foothold on the sidewalk. I'm reunited with Dianne and Yvonne at last.

Yvonne reiterates her commitment to our care. "We'll get one of those taxis to stop. Want me to take your suitcase? There's a better chance at a taxi just up the street. You just take your time. You need to stop and rest? No hurry."

Yvonne and I carry on a truncated conversation as we slowly make our way up the block. I begin to tell her about my Parkinson's disease and the current failure of usually effective medicine. "Your wife told me," she interjects.

She repeats her earlier offers and reassurances. "Do you need to rest? Do you want me to wheel your suitcase? You sure you don't want me to take it from you? We're in no hurry," she repeats.

"Thanks, but I need to manage the suitcase myself," I reply.

Yvonne appears puzzled by my rejection of her offer.

I tell her, "If I quit now, there's no telling what else I may give up on."

"You givin' up don't look real likely to me," she comments.

We finally reach the point Yvonne has chosen to make our stand. She instructs us to wait as she steps off the curb, hand raised, seeking the attention of passing taxis. Though we are no longer in close competition with other ride-seekers, most of the passing cabs are already occupied. The first two taxis Yvonne stops refuse to take us. The trip is probably too short to offer a worthwhile fare. She is momentarily set back but undaunted.

"I'm gonna get one of these guys to take you. Don't you worry!" she declares, remaining vigilant for an available, unoccupied vehicle. A bit more time passes. True to her word, Yvonne has snared and commandeered a taxi. She is giving direction to its now-captive driver. She hurriedly bundles Dianne into the rear seat of the waiting cab. As Yvonne next takes my arm and guides me to the taxi's rear door, she commands the driver to retrieve and transfer my luggage from curbside to the vehicle's trunk. Reaching for my wallet, I implore her, "Let me give you my business card. Someday, you may need help." She declines my offer. Promise made. Promise kept.

Dianne and I are now cocooned in the relative safety of this New York City taxi. As the cab merges with the tightly packed traffic, I catch a last glimpse of Yvonne. She's back on the sidewalk, monitoring our progress, confirming the successful transfer of responsibility for our care. Though she is gazing in our direction, our eyes no longer meet. Grateful as we are, we have now moved beyond the orbit of the generosity, compassion, and unbidden kindness of this stranger. A wordless sigh of relief expresses our thanks.

Pumped

It's a given that one's sexuality is usually awkward to disclose and discuss. That said, even in the most ordinary of circumstances, advancing age brings a predictable decline in perceived capacity to evoke erotic interest in others. Perhaps this is embedded in the evolutionary biology of our species. Maybe it's just a cruel twist of fate. Add Parkinson's disease to the mix, and you have a compounding effect on your feelings of attractiveness.

It's hard to imagine an aged, sometimes unsteady individual as powerfully appealing. Virility is difficult to picture in one who may be shuffling, tremulous, or precarious in balance. The sense of oneself as sexually desirable easily evaporates. So it probably comes as no surprise that eroticized interest or attention becomes especially precious and memorable to someone with Parkinson's disease.

My neurologist is among the most significant women in my life, second only to my wife. I am blessed to receive her expert and compassionate medical care. Exercise is an important part of Dr. Jill's therapy plan for managing my Parkinson's disease. She and my wife are close allies in a mission to assure my maximum involvement in physical activity.

Dianne has historically been our family cheerleader for new recreational ventures. Some months ago, consistent with her self-appointed mission, she learned of a new and highly touted weight-training regimen at our gym. It's somewhat brashly labeled Body Pump. Dianne lobbies me to join her in this new strength-training foray. Her incessant entreaties finally convince me.

Over the ensuing weeks, we become regular participants in this group activity, consisting of a variety of weight-training routines designed to tone and strengthen muscles. They are all set to loud, pulsating music and led by one or another of the facility's fit female training staff. It's as if Arnold Schwarzenegger has been joined with John Travolta in female form. Much to my surprise, my periodic snide comments notwithstanding, I have come to enjoy the activity.

Given my self-perceived diminished attractiveness, I am both startled and gratified by an encounter with a couple of friends. Leaving the spa one morning, I pause to chat with fellow participants Linda and Barbara. Barbara innocently volunteers an observation.

"The body pump class is really making a difference in your body. I haven't seen much of your lower
body, but your upper body shows much more muscle
tone."

Barbara's unbidden assessment and Linda's quick
agreement surprise me. Unable to immediately digest
the flattering feedback, and mildly embarrassed, I go
for an easy laugh.

"Well, I'm sure we could work out something for
you to see a lot more of my lower body," I respond.

Both women laugh. I treasure this increasingly
rare moment of verbal flirting. Who would have
predicted this delicious consequence, this surprise
reawakening of savored yet dormant feeling, resulting from the collaboration between my doctor and
my wife? With this kind of surprise outcome potentially in store, I may have to take their future advice
even more seriously than I already do.

Hell on Wheels

I can't recall the precise moment when I decided to take the next "step." Perhaps I was motivated by being far from home in a new and unexplored place. Dianne and I had driven to the Southern California coast for a brief vacation. Night had fallen by the time we were settled in our rented cottage. After two days on the road, we were tired and hungry. Since we hadn't yet stocked up on groceries, we opted for dinner at a neighborhood restaurant. Nevertheless, within a block and a half of setting out on foot, my walking began to deteriorate. I'd been attentive to my medication schedule, but the most recent dose was not working well. Though the short trek had become more laborious than anticipated, we muddled through. Shortly after reaching the restaurant, the medicine began to take effect.

Later that night while Dianne slept, I began surfing the internet. An ad popped up on my computer screen:

"... revolutionary ... Freedom Rollator ... lightest [one] available ... many unique features ... weighs only 11 pounds ... attractive burgundy color ... 250-pound weight capacity ... $99 ... free shipping ... no tax ..."

Given my dread of prematurely abandoning parts of my life to Parkinson's disease, I'd resisted mechanical assistance. The use of such devices, I believed, would inevitably lead to increasing reliance on them instead of on myself. A decade after being diagnosed, I was succumbing to the progression of the disease. I had to face the fact that I now needed something to aid my mobility, to back me up when pharmaceuticals failed. But what should that be? How would it help? What impact would it have on those around me? Enter the Freedom Rollator, "the lightest Rollator available."

I quickly placed an order for a burgundy-colored model. It arrived via UPS at about the same time that we returned home from vacation. I immediately removed the rollator from its shipping carton, set about doing the minimal assembly required and adjusted the fit to my size. There it was, my collapsible four-wheeled, hand-braked, burgundy, mechanical-mobility device, with ergonomically contoured hand grips, padded seat and backrest, and storage compartment. With its broad, well-balanced four-wheel base, low center of gravity, and customizable height adjustments, it seemed up to the task of assuring some degree of movement when my medicine failed to do so.

After assembling my new wheels, I immediately try them out. I have good upper-body strength and quickly master its basic operation, firmly seizing both hand grips, fingers on the hand-brake contours. I cautiously step forward and allow the device to advance on its rolling wheels. I soon discover that it can also be operated with its rear wheels locked by lifting the fixed rear wheels just off the ground and pushing it forward on its free and swiveling front wheels. I'm curious to see what else it can do. So, I begin experimenting with it as a scooter.

With a hand on one of the hand-grip/brake levers, I grasp the backrest with my other hand, hoist my right knee onto the padded seat, and use my extended left leg to propel myself across the full length of our living-room floor. It's like riding the scooter I'd known as a child. I feel like a kid with a new toy as I fly across the room. Dianne appears concerned with my potential recklessness. But I'm caught up in the exuberance of my playful maiden voyage. I pay her no mind. Thankfully, no disastrous crash ensues. But I soon realize that mastering the operating technique is the easy part: bringing the rollator out in public will be the hard part, the part I fear.

I soon have an opportunity to put my fearful fantasy to the test.

Our town of 5,000 is home to The Harwood Museum of Art and its 125-seat Arthur Bell Auditorium. It's a venue that hosts a variety of programs ranging from chamber music to jazz to poetry readings. Dianne and I are regular patrons.

One sunny late-February afternoon, my new Freedom Rollator in the car, we arrive early at the Harwood. Parking close to the museum's entry, we avoid the facility's rough entry-area surfaces. I'm walking well and have no immediate need for assistance. The rollator is along just in case.

Once beyond the entryway's massive antique doors, we make our way directly to the auditorium. The few earlier-arriving patrons are scattered among the various levels of the room's stadium-style seating. I park my wheels off to the side on the entry level in the hope that it will not interfere with the flow of people. The auditorium gradually fills. As the program begins, I am distracted by thoughts of the reaction that will greet the public presence of my wheels at the performance's conclusion. Several friends and acquaintances are in the audience. I am confident someone will ask.

But what shall I say or do? Crack a joke? Deflect interest or concern? Adopt a thousand-yard stare? Refuse to make eye contact with any who would take note? These thoughts compete with my focus on the music.

The performance ends to a standing ovation. After a couple of minutes, the applause dies down and the audience, already on its feet, slowly shuffles toward the stepped aisles at each side of the auditorium. Moving rather normally, I am carried along in the logjam of exiting patrons. I peel away from the line and retrieve my waiting wheels. As I rejoin the slow-moving herd, I push my rollator before me. I'm intent on proceeding as efficiently as possible, avoiding eye contact as I go.

As the crowd advances, its flow constricts at a choke point near the auditorium exit. Ann, a friend of several years, notes my wheels and stops me. "What's happened? Have you hurt yourself?"

"No. It's just backup for when I get beyond the medicine's ability to handle my Parkinson's symptoms and I can't move so well," I reply.

"Oh, I thought you might have been injured," she says.

"No, it's just Parkinson's," I say.

A few weeks later, the pattern repeats itself — this time at the town's somewhat larger 300-seat performance venue. The gallery lobby is filled with eager fans. I am again accompanied by my rollator. Kandace and Gunther, friends of several years, are among the waiting throng. Kandace and I have casually discussed Parkinson's disease on prior occasions. She immediately notices the presence of my rollator.

"What's this?" she says, gesturing in the direction of my wheels. "Have things gotten worse?"

"Perhaps. It's a progressive thing. No dramatic change. Just more frequent times when my drugs might not be working like I'd hoped. I've got this thing along as a kind of backup."

"Oh, that's better. When I saw you with it, I thought you might have suddenly gotten much worse."

"Well, that's one of the problems with this thing. It's impossible not to notice it. It startles and concerns friends. It's like waving a red flag or carrying a sign," I respond.

"I see what you mean. If you hadn't explained, I would have assumed the worst."

Though I know Kandace well enough to confide in her further, I'll save that for some other place and time. For now, I've chosen to keep to myself my concern that in agreeing to use mechanical devices like this rollator, I may be hastening the day when I lose independent ability. Ultimately, my embrace of this mechanical assist saddles me with dual concerns: needlessly alarming my friends and feeding my ongoing worry that its use may compromise my independence. It remains an unresolved dilemma. If only they really made one of those sci-fi invisibility machines. Thus far, the only way I've found to allay the concern evoked by its sudden appearance is to preempt any look of alarm with a declaration of its mechanical insurance status. Perhaps I could just attach a banner to it reading something like what I had said in response to my friend Ann: "Not to worry! It's just Parkinson's disease, that persistent pain in the ass."

Although I am dismissive of my friends' expressions of concern for my well-being, I do privately worry that my use of mechanical aids may compromise my eventual ability to move on my own. As for that, we shall see.

One of the Hardest Things

Having dear friends has always felt like an unqualified blessing. But these days, it sometimes feels like a curse. This fact of my current social life was painfully underscored one recent cold midwinter night.

With a major snowstorm bearing down on us, Dianne and I head for a live theater performance. As luck would have it, the play is being staged on the second floor of a historic building: The Mural Room of Taos's old county courthouse. With treasured WPA-era justice-themed frescoes adorning this courtroom of yesteryear, it's a setting that many cherish. In the abstract, I share their love of this place.

But a problem with this venerated structure is that its design predates ADA-mandated construction codes. It just wasn't planned for people with impaired mobility—people like me. There is no protection from inclement weather until one is almost inside the building's designated north-side Mural Room entrance. The restrooms are located down an outdoor flight of stairs and across an alley. There are no elevators. Limited close-proximity parking was an afterthought.

Driving into the building's rear parking area, we quickly note that the few handicapped-designated parking spaces are occupied. Though the parking lot's surface is already snow packed, the approaching storm has not yet hit. Spotting a not-too-distant space, we pull in and head for the building's rear entrance.

Passing the outdoor restrooms, we see a sign announcing, "Winter closing at 5 p.m." It's now nearing 7 p.m., and I'm already feeling the need for relief. I wonder how I will make it through the two-hour performance. My concern is compounded by the fact that my medicine is not working effectively. Nevertheless, I proceed up the outdoor staircase.

Already inside, Dianne has claimed our tickets. Typically, I'd be delighted with the front-row-center seats. But not tonight. Their location requires me to get from the rear of the room to its very front, and I am already having some difficulty walking. Ordinarily, I would have brought along my rollator. However, given the venue's unaccommodating design and the snow-packed parking area, there was no way to get the rollator from my car, up the stairs, into the theater, up to our front-row seats, and back to the car again at the performance's end.

As planned, Dianne and I are among the first arrivals. It's still half an hour before curtain time. I unsteadily make my way along the rows created by the temporary arrangement of some 60 folding chairs. We take our seats and peruse the program, commenting on its contents from time to time, while later-arriving ticket holders filter into the room. We greet those we know. Occupying the seats to our right are Martha and Helen. To our left are Tom and Marie.

It's finally curtain time for a play that is by turns comedy and drama. But first a series of standard announcements: thanks are offered to sponsors, admonitions are issued regarding electronic devices, and apologies made for the rear-alley restroom unavailability. We are further advised that a single restroom will be available within the building at intermission. I'm grateful for the possibility, but unclear as to how I will reach it.

The play's first act concludes in an hour. It's now intermission, and I'm trapped in ambivalence regarding my ability to access the now urgently required restroom.

A single restroom for the entire audience and cast? Will there be a mad dash for it? Exactly where in the building is it located? Can I get there? Can I wait? Do I need Dianne's help? There's at least another hour to go. So much effort demanded for something so routine!

Dianne offers her arm. Fortunately, there is only one other person waiting to use the facility. Seeing my need for assistance, this stranger defers to my perceived greater need.

"Why don't you get ahead of me?" she says.

"Are you sure that's OK?"

"Sure. Go on. I'm all right," she answers.

I'm in the restroom at last. I would have found it difficult to wait much longer. I'm thankful for this urgently required relief, and once again grateful for the kindness of strangers.

Pit stop concluded, I haltingly (but unaided) make my way back to my seat. I suspect Tom and Marie have observed the entire process. As with some other friends, Tom has never seen me in this condition.

The play finally ends, and Tom and Marie are on their feet. Tom comments, "Being a psychologist, you must have loved the play."

Here's where it gets difficult, both physically and emotionally. Much as I like Tom, I'm hoping that he and Marie will not linger. I barely acknowledge his effort to engage. While the play was progressing, so was the snowstorm, and so were my movement difficulties. If Tom and Marie hang around, I know he's going to want to help. His good-natured generosity is part of the reason I like him. However, short of carrying me to my car, which he would likely be physically capable of doing and which I certainly could never permit, there is nothing he nor anybody else can do. The result of this kindness, concern, and generosity becomes an additional encumbrance for me. It brings the dual burden of concentrating on moving my body while simultaneously responding to the helpless, frustrated, powerless feelings that I know I will see frozen on the faces and etched in the eyes of would-be helpers.

Finally exiting the building, we find the snowstorm in full fury. It has already dumped several inches of fresh snow. I must get down the flight of stairs to the alley behind the building, cross to the parking area, and to my car. As I reach the bottom of the stairs, Tom and Marie have emerged from the building and are coming down the snow-covered stairway. They appear to be heading in a similar direction.

Tom calls out, "Bob, can I give you a hand? Would you like me to drive your car around?"

"Thanks, Tom, but I can manage. I'll just be a bit slow," I respond.

"Are you sure?" he persists.

"Yes. I'm sure. We'll be OK."

"Well, all right then, if you're sure."

Out of the corner of my eye, I can see them slowly walking toward their car. I don't want to look at them too directly for fear that I will see their worried concern.

It's a difficult thing for me to explain, and perhaps even more difficult for friends to hear and accept. However, it actually makes life easier for me if they suppress their undeniably generous inclination to "help," and do no more than I request. Permitting or encouraging caring friends to do things for me that I can do for myself, my obvious struggle notwithstanding, won't be any favor to me. Dianne understands this. Though she may at times appear to be standing idly by as I try to move my legs, she is likely doing as I have asked. She is allowing me to labor, as I must. Similarly, though my dear friends would very much wish to make things better for me, they can't. Their anxious concern for my well-being continues to be one of the very hardest things for me to manage.

Pride Before the Fall

"No falls. Ever!" These words are prominently posted on my doctor's office wall. Since falls are the second most common cause of hospitalization in Parkinson's patients, every visit includes Dr. Jill's routine query.

"Any falls since your last appointment?" she asks. Her insistent focus on this possibility reflects the lurking danger. Nevertheless, I'd been completely unprepared for what happened on that beautiful, clear, cool, summer morning in the high desert.

Dianne and I are preparing for an early bike ride prior to the Sunday church service we plan to attend. Pressed for time, I undertake a bit of seemingly benign though forbidden multitasking. Manipulating my battery-powered toothbrush, I step beyond our bedroom doors onto our backyard flagstone patio. I've been watching over our tomato crop for weeks, and am unable to restrain my curiosity at the prospect of finally being able to harvest some ripe fruit.

Making my way past the garden's wire-mesh barrier, I continue the two-minute tooth-brushing routine prescribed by my dental hygienist. Whirring toothbrush in hand, I methodically place its spinning brush head at each successive tooth. Simultaneously, I press my body against the stucco wall that defines the narrow garden's perimeter, careful to avoid trampling a row of emerging green beans. Then, maneuvering around a flourishing lilac bush, I reach the caged tomato plants. To my delight, they are fully leafed out and laden with fruit. I press on, foot placements in selected voids between the plants. Moving among the plants, I note their ripening progress for relay to Dianne.

I conclude my morning agriculture rounds amid wild, lush, randomly rooted, thorn-encrusted raspberry canes located in the furthest reaches of the garden. Inspection complete, I reverse course, thread my way back through the tomatoes, past the beans, back to the wire-mesh point of entry. Tooth-brushing routine still in progress, I next make my way to the gravel surface surrounding the hot tub and on toward the patio furniture. But suddenly I'm falling. I've snagged the toe of my shoe in a gap between flagstones. Balance unexpectedly compromised, I crash into a heavy, glass-topped table. The considerable force of my landing topples it. Lacking any means to dampen my momentum,

I make a hard landing — smack on the stone patio. Every possible part of my body except my head has made contact with the unforgiving flagstone.

Given my active lifestyle, I'm no stranger to falls. On the tennis court, I've trained myself to hold onto my racquet while falling, using it as a skid and protecting my hands from abrasion by the gritty surface. But the current fall is one for my personal record book. Writhing on the ground in agony, I've wrenched my back; peeled back a bloody section of skin on my left inner forearm; bruised my right fore-arm, right shoulder, and left knee; and skinned my right knee. All has transpired in a single, sudden, careless instant.

I lay there moaning, unable to rise. Dianne hears the backyard commotion and is quickly at my side.

"What happened?" she says.

"Slammed into the table. Twisted my back. Arm's bleeding. Knee and shoulder hurt. Didn't hit my head. Flagstone gap caught my toe. Tripped!"

"What do you need me to do? Should I help you up?"

"Just let me lay here. Be OK in a minute."

"I guess the bike ride's off."

"Won't be able to manage that."

"Tell me what you need me to do," Dianne says, while keeping an alarmed eye fixed on me. She continues her watchful waiting while collecting the still spinning toothbrush and returning the disarrayed furniture to its original position.

I lay there for several more minutes, thankful that although I'm in pain, I don't appear to have suffered permanent injury. I make my way back into the house, attend to my bloody forearm, and shower and dress for church. The irony surrounding my seemingly unlikely accident dominates my thoughts. A week ago, I had scaled a 13,161-foot mountain without injury or incident. On the preceding day, I climbed an extension ladder to our roof to clear debris deposited by our large trees, also without mishap. Yet, I have just been brought dangerously low in the most banal of circumstances. Walking on relatively level ground in my own backyard, I had been oblivious to the existence of threat or danger.

Some hours later, Dianne insists that we have "the conversation." With tears of fear in her eyes, she issues an unequivocal declaration.

"You've just got to stop doing things like this! You know you can't do more than one thing at a time. Be honest with Dr. Jill about these falls at your next visit. No making light of them and telling her everything is fine. Everything is not fine. You can't keep doing these things. You can't keep up this pretense that you can do as you please. What will it be like in the future?"

"I didn't think I was doing anything especially

dangerous — just walking across the patio. I didn't mean to scare you."

"I'm not talking about you scaring me. I'm talking about you doing things that aren't safe."

Though I'm sure her analysis is correct, I'm still fixated on the irony of the mountain climb and roof ascent so recently accomplished without major mishap or injury. Both involved situations in which I was fully alert to dangers. In those two manifestly dangerous situations, I was fully focused on the single task at hand and on none other. But walking across my own backyard, my guard down, I'd been oblivious to the presence of threat. I presumed that I could relax my vigilance, complicate my focus, and do more than a single thing at a time.

It's been a sobering episode. My own actions put me at risk, orchestrating injury and pain. Where's the line? When does accepting some risk produce the fullest life experience? When is it rash and foolhardy? I wish I had the answer.

Though chastened, I'm still in search of the bright line separating unthinking recklessness from acceptable risk. One thing's for sure: I don't want to be another faceless data point connecting Parkinson's disease, falls, and hospitalization.

An Expert's Touch

Though I can't remember how I found her, I adore this woman. She's in her fifties, close to six feet tall, slender, muscular, in superb athletic condition, and a martial-arts competitor. I've dubbed her "the exercise Nazi" in feigned protest of her insistence that I follow a regimen of regular, intense physical exercise. I trust and depend on her. She is my vital, reliable link to a full life. Despite my resistance to dependency, I would without hesitation follow this woman anywhere. She is Doctor Jill. She is my doctor.

I see Jill every three months. Though the drive is two and a half hours from our Taos home to her Albuquerque office, I would travel any distance and endure any inconvenience to remain in this acclaimed specialist's care. I have no idea why she chose this professional path, but her practice is limited to people with movement disorders, people like me. I owe my surprisingly rich life to her nuanced management of the pharmaceutical cocktails on which I depend, and to her management of me.

From Jill's appearance and manner, I wouldn't have suspected her impressive achievements in academic medicine, nor even identified her as a physician. She just doesn't look or act the part: no white lab coat, not even business-casual attire for this woman. Instead, she's likely to be dressed in functional athletic clothing, like she's just come from working out at a gym.

And then there's the matter of her office structure and staffing — no receptionist, nurse, secretary, scheduler, or any other human assistant. Jill fields her own phone calls, schedules her own appointments, runs her own copies, writes her own notes, and does her own billing. No one greets us upon arrival, not even to confirm that we are in fact at her office. We are met, at best, by some scribbled note posted on her consulting-room door, suggesting that the doctor is most likely in, probably running late, and will be with us as soon as possible.

Her practice is a no-frills, pure doctor-patient collaboration. All of Jill's energy seems reserved not for appearances but for adept, focused, effective care. Quirky though the context of her ministrations may be, she's by far the best neurologist I've ever seen.

As Dianne and I drive the 135 miles to Jill's Albuquerque office, I ruminate in silence. I know that Jill has always managed to tinker effectively with my medication. I struggle to remain optimistic but can't banish the fear that this past three-month period, when my symptoms were well-medicated and well-managed, might have been my best time.

We arrive for my scheduled visit some fifteen minutes early. This is a compromise. Dianne prefers not to be early. I, on the other hand, am loath to chance missing even a second of my time with Jill. I'd be here even earlier. For me, Jill has near magical powers. Her calm, kind, matter-of-fact confidence in devising a path through my maze of frustrating symptoms instills hope in me. I'm probably some 20 years older than Jill. Perhaps she touches me at an unconscious level as if she were a nurturing daughter or a younger sister, deeply invested in the fullness of my life. We take our seats in the bland waiting area outside her consulting-room door and hope for the best.

Jill is, as usual, running a bit late. This evokes some anxiety in me.

"Are you sure she's here?" asks Dianne, giving voice to my unspoken fear.

Surely she hasn't forgotten? We haven't miscommunicated, have we?

Jill finally appears in the now-open doorway to her consulting room. I'm immediately relieved. She seems almost as pleased to see me as I am to see her. She motions us to enter. Her exam/consultation space is small, cramped, and disorganized looking. Files are piled on the floor and on most available horizontal surfaces, but I couldn't care less about the aesthetics. A few well-chosen mottoes and epigrams are posted on the walls. There is an image of Jill outfitted in karate regalia, in combat pose, samurai-type sword in hand, as if battling the Parkinson's beast. Photographs of family members are posted among those of others, probably patients, engaged in unlikely physical activities or as recognition of significant accomplishments.

As we begin, Jill is locating files, updating my prescriptions, issuing instructions, offering useful printed information. While she takes my measure, she may simultaneously engage us in some conversation regarding her teenage daughters, her passion for skiing and martial arts, or her impending orthopedic surgery. Yet I never doubt that Jill is focused on me, watching every move I make, listening to each word I utter, gauging the status of my disease.

Jill invites me to update her on the current state of my Parkinson's symptoms. I lead with the good news of the physical activities in which I've participated, saving whatever binds or grinds I've struggled with for later. It falls to Dianne to prompt me regarding the bad news I must also share.

"Are you going to tell Jill about the falls and the freeze-ups?" Dianne asks.

I gradually relate the rest of my story. I must share the full picture for Jill to devise my best treatment, but I'm battling my wish to not be a burden or a source of worry to those who care for me. I'm also resisting painting a picture that might impair my determined optimism. Jill has seen me at my best and at my very worst. But no matter what the details of my story for the day, she listens patiently, calmly, and unemotionally, never rushing or interrupting me. She's in analysis and problem-solving mode and will reliably spit out a best solution to whatever I've presented.

In anticipation of our visit, Dianne has had some concern regarding my use of the most recent of the five Parkinson's medicines I now take each day.

"Tell Jill how you're taking the new medicine," she says.

"Dianne is referring to the half-tablet of Sinemet," I respond.

"How have you been using it?" Jill asks.

"Well, if I'm anticipating some active recreation — like skiing, tennis, biking, or hiking — I'll probably take half a Sinemet about half an hour before I start ... to give me a bit of a boost."

"That's fine," Jill says.

"And if we're out somewhere and I just start to freeze up, I'll take a half then," I add.

"That's OK," she says.

"I've never taken more than the two tablets on any day."

"He's taking the medicine like he should," says Jill.

Her clear, direct, quiet reassurance has at least temporarily eased Dianne's anxiety. We can now move on.

Neurological exams typically don't involve much laying on of hands, and Jill's is no exception. She'll watch me closely while directing me to stand, walk across the room, maintain my balance as she presses against my shoulders, or resist her strong arms and gentle hands pushing my horizontally extended arms down to my sides.

Having covered the minutiae of my pharmaceutical and medical management, our time together has now come to its end. She concludes our visit with an unselfconscious, gestured invitation to an *abrazo,* a warm, affectionate, farewell embrace, wordlessly declaring that she is not some bloodless technician. Nor is she merely my physician. She's a caring and compassionate fellow human being, a technically sophisticated friend with the courage to put aside the protective armor of her professional role and allow her humanity to show. With this parting physical contact, Jill symbolically declares that humanity trumps orthodoxy.

As I reach for her, Jill subtly adjusts for the difference in our heights, lightly wrapping her much longer arms around me. Her touch validates my belief that she will remain committed to my care over the months of separation ahead. I, too, will carry her in my thoughts and in my heart until we meet again. Could I possibly be in any better hands than those of my dear doctor, Jill?

"Grim"

"In a dozen years, your life will be grim!" This abrupt declaration from a neurologist is seared in my memory. I'd intended the bravado of my unaccompanied diagnostic consultation to dampen my burgeoning concern. Yet I'm stunned by this doctor's unequivocal pronouncement. It's as if I've been kicked in the gut. I'm shaken and disoriented by this terse prognosis. Struggling to maintain my composure, I stammer pro forma thanks for his directness.

Then 63 years old, physically fit, and in otherwise good health, I'm told that I have Parkinson's disease, a chronic, progressive, incurable neurological disorder that will severely reorder the tone and tenor of my future ... for the worse. I've drawn a proverbial black bean in life's lottery. Though deeply disturbed by the news, I'd pressed for a glimpse of what lay ahead in this uncharted territory. I was groping for a sound prediction of the life that would be mine.

Exiting the medical office, I am awash in confusion and uncertainty. The doctor's pronouncement ricochets in the recesses of my mind. "Grim," was what he had said. This was the key operative word. But what will grim look like? How incapacitated will I become? How soon will I reach the end of the line? Will mine be a life be worth living?

As with most Parkinson's cases, there were probably clues that I had the disease long before it was formally diagnosed. In hindsight, this comes into sharper focus. "Pick up your feet!" Dianne would sometimes say to me during morning walks. It was as if I were some lazy adolescent, indifferently dragging his heels. Looking back, I wonder if this foot dragging was an early sign of the disease. When a mild hand tremor appeared, I knew that I needed to seek medical consultation. I already assumed I had Parkinson's disease. A visit with my internist and subsequent referral to this neurology specialist confirmed my private suspicions.

As it turns out, the "grim" prognosis was incorrect. Though generally knowledgeable, this initial neurologist had no baseline for predicting this highly variable disease's progression in my specific case. On average, his "grim" time-line prophesy might be accurate. In my case, it appears incorrect.

I remain physically active. However, without multiple doses of several different medications each day, I would be profoundly immobilized. I respond well to available pharmaceuticals, receiving therapeutic benefit without unacceptable side effects. If someone with a chronic, progressive, incurable disease can be thought of as lucky, I'm lucky. All in my cohort are not so fortunate.

The neurologist's "grim" prediction ultimately provoked unanticipated consequences. I reacted to his prophecy as if it were unimpeachable. I behaved with an urgency befitting the anticipated truncation of my life. When opportunities came my way, I accepted them without hesitation. When new ventures were not forthcoming, I created them. I was convinced that I was running out of time, and I reacted in a manner consistent with that belief.

If I was invited to join some board of directors, I barely gave acceptance a second thought. If I asked to take on some position of responsibility, I threw myself into the task with a gusto that I was certain wouldn't exist for long. I was determined to live life to its near-manic fullest before running out of the time prophesied. I was neither selective nor judicious in my investment of time and energy.

Dianne would regularly protest my innumerable extracurricular involvements and evening absences. "Why do you want to spend time on that? Another evening meeting? Do they always have to meet at night? How late will you be? We've never lived like this. You're always gone!"

Her complaints seemed like unwarranted, controlling, critical intrusions that could potentially limit my life's already waning opportunities. I routinely waved her off. It never occurred to me that she might be saying she needed more of me. I was, after all, running out of time, or so I believed.

Then, a crisis drastically reordered the mobility-impairment vector in our marriage. Dianne had been out skiing with a mutual friend when she hit some ski-slope crud, invisible in the day's flat light. Her ensuing fall resulted in a broken ankle and the immediate reorientation of our roles. Dianne now became the one with the most pressing mobility challenges and need for assistance. With her left ankle in a rigid boot for many weeks, I scrupulously took up the challenge of her care. She was either on crutches or in a wheel chair. I became her driver and her aide, dutifully attending to her suddenly impaired mobility yet simultaneously maintaining my involvement in the multiple activities that had become my new norm.

Dianne had suffered an obvious, significant physical injury. But she had also sustained an emotional wound that I utterly failed to notice. Dianne's ankle injury had dramatically altered her life, keeping her from the physical activity she thrived on. But blinded by my own Parkinson's preoccupation,

I was oblivious to the psychological injury she had also suffered. For over forty years, detecting and treating psychological injuries had been my career, yet I'd been unmindful of this in my own wife. As if this had anything to do with logic, I was focused on a false dichotomy: a broken ankle is routinely cured. You ultimately recover. Parkinson's disease has no cure. You never recover. I'd take a broken bone over Parkinson's any day! What was the big deal?

After some weeks, Dianne's cast finally came off, but things were nowhere near back to normal. Along with some long-standing, mostly patched-over relationship fissures, my hyperactivity had blinded me to her emotional needs, provoking a crisis in our marriage. In my fixation on what I thought was the unrelenting ebbing of my life's quality, I neglected the very heart of it. It was as if I had imagined that the diagnosis granted me license to disregard what was most precious to me.

Weathering the relationship storm, we proceeded to put our life together... back together. Healing relationship wounds was agonizing. Though my career had taught me that relationship struggles are most always jointly authored, I had control of only my contribution to our marriage's near demise. This, I was determined to remedy. Though counterintuitive, I could slow down and live my life sanely, preserving the marriage I treasured. The Parkinson's diagnosis never bestowed any emotional immunity, no carte blanche for insensitivity or irresponsibility.

Coming to grips with my role in putting our marriage at risk remains a work in progress. I gradually grow accustomed to a more measured approach to the life that is mine. I'm still determined to live it fully; but with a more accurate view of my future and of our relationship's vulnerability, I don't need to throw myself at all possibilities. It's likely to be calmer, more satisfying, and saner this way. While I don't have all the time in the world, there is still time...time enough for a life worth living.

Timing

Though not routinely a life-threatening condition, Parkinson's disease does in fact threaten some of life's most basic pleasures. Take, for example, the universal desire to share good food with dear friends. Parkinson's disease persistently complicates it. Given my three-hour medication schedule, there is a never-ending review on any given day as to when meals may be best timed to fit my medication-driven constraints. Normal people do not live this way.

Ingesting protein blocks the uptake of the primary medicine I require every three hours to gain some semblance of movement. For optimal mobility, I must avoid protein during the hour preceding a dose and within the hour following a dose. This limits eating protein to the middle hour in each three-hour time block. If I eat outside this time interval, I must limit myself to food that contains zero protein.

My medication schedule typically begins at either four or five in the morning, depending on the

activities I've set for that day. If I start my medicine at four, meals containing protein can be con-
sumed in the one-hour intervals between five and
six, eight and nine, eleven and noon, two and three
in the afternoon, five and six, and eight to nine in
the evening. The pattern shifts one hour later if I
begin medication at 5 a.m.

Dianne recently joked about the rigidity of my
meal schedule: "You're a bit like an infant on a
three-hour feeding schedule!" she said.

"It does fit the pattern," I replied.

This complicating fact of my social life played
out over a meal with friends. "Tim" and "Maddi"
would soon be our neighbors, and they wanted us
to see their current residence prior to its sale. So
they invited us to dinner. It seemed a relaxed way
to enjoy their company, so we readily accepted.
The invitation was for 6 p.m. on a weeknight, and
included "Jan," a mutual friend. She lives nearby
and has been to Maddi and Tim's. We arrange to
pick her up and have her guide us there.

The day of the dinner party arrives. It is atyp-
ically dreary. Rain has been falling since morning.
We collect Jan and head for Tim and Maddi's, ten
minutes away. Traffic moves slowly through the rain.

We finally make our way down the last stretch
of rutted and waterlogged dirt road leading to the
house. Since the invitation was for 6 p.m., I assume

that dinner will probably be served at about seven. I've adjusted my medication schedule to fit the anticipated timing of dinner, look forward to the prospect of an enjoyable, convivial meal, and expect to be homeward bound while my medicine is still working.

On arrival, things are proceeding as assumed. Our hosts offer wine and cocktails, and I'm able to walk about fairly normally as Maddi conducts a tour of her inviting, thick-walled, adobe home. The old house's interior has a contrasting contemporary look and feel, reinforced by the uncrowded hanging of abstract paintings likely selected by our artist-hostess.

Anticipating constricted passageways and uneven floor surfaces that would render the rollator useless, I have not brought my wheels along. My prediction is accurate as to the house's narrow doorways, barrier-constituting thresholds, and slightly uneven floor surfaces. Dianne declares this house to be the nicest Taos home she has seen. It has not, however, been designed with impaired mobility in mind.

Wine glasses in hand, we are ushered into a high-ceilinged sitting area. The room is furnished with two comfortable cream-colored couches, separated by a large, square, glass-topped coffee table. On the table are a plate of shrimp, a cheese board, and a bowl of roasted almonds. Now in a protein-avoidance time period, they are currently off limits for me. The almonds, we later learn, are from

Maddi's mother's California farm.

We settle into the couches as Maddi relates the house's history. Though the others seem relaxed and comfortable with the pace of the unfolding visit, I'm starting to worry about the time. The conversation ranges from opinions on Southwestern architecture to the nature of art. I'm only paying partial attention. My furtive and hopefully unobtrusive glances at my watch reveal that it's approaching seven. Yet, there seems to be no rush to get on with serving dinner, which I'd anticipated for about seven o'clock. It should be on the table by now.

My uncertainty about our eventual dinner hour growing, I begin munching on the shrimp and almonds before us. I'm thinking this could be it for me as far as dinner is concerned. Tim and Maddi are checking on the progress of the oven-roasting pork loin and issue regular bulletins regarding its progress.

"I usually do this on the outdoor grill," Tim announces. "But, since it's raining, I thought I'd do it in the oven. I've never done it this way."

Having roasted and grilled many a pork loin, I wish I could march into the kitchen and get the job done. As with many Parkinson's patients, my sense of smell is compromised, so that eliminates a major clue as to the progress of cooking.

Following several additional oven checks and

accompanying bulletins by our hosts, Jan is a bit impatient.

"Do you have a meat thermometer?" she inquires.

Dianne follows up, "You know, one of those with the blue plastic sheaths."

"One of the instant-read ones," I chime in.

More fruitless oven checks ensue.

It's now nearing eight, and my concern with the timing of dinner has reached its zenith. Things are obviously not going to work as hoped. By nine, it's unlikely that my medicine will be working.

Finally, sometime after eight, our hosts issue the long-awaited announcement that "dinner is served!"

The dining room is just beyond a nearby narrow doorway. I'm not yet having any disabling movement problems. While I'm still able to do so, I immediately rise from the deep couch and walk the short distance to my designated place at the dining-room table.

As dinner proceeds, I'm distracted by knowledge of the likely difficulty I'll have at the evening's end. Maddi is seated to my immediate left and is not very familiar with Parkinson's disease. She asks some standard questions.

"How long have you had it? Can it be cured?"

She'll probably learn more than enough by the end of the evening, I'm thinking.

Jan has made dessert to accompany the meal. She is disappointed that her whipping cream has somehow refused to whip up. It coats the pumpkin pie in a thin liquid, sweet and white. Ann, Maddi, and Dianne are all visual artists. Appearance matters. As for me, the current disappointment seems in fitting company with the roast that wouldn't roast and my legs that will likely fail to walk.

It's now after nine. Dianne is seated next to me and whispers, "We should probably go. Can you walk?"

"Well, we're about to find out," I respond, as I slowly slide my chair back from the table.

My impairment is obvious as I stand. By now, my immobility has become a group concern.

"Would you like me to drive?" Jan asks.

"No. Once I get to the car, I'll be OK," I respond.

Ann appears unconvinced.

"How about letting me drive you all home?" Maddi offers.

"He'll be able to drive once he gets to the car," insists Dianne.

The rain is still falling as a group effort develops to help me out into the night and to my car.

Finally in the driver's seat, I start the engine, put the car in gear, slowly pull out of the driveway onto the puddled dirt road, and head back through the steady rain toward town. As I drive, I contemplate future dinners with friends. It's not uncommon in my age cohort for dinner invitations to include queries regarding dietary restrictions. I'll need to find a way to let prospective hosts know that while there is nothing I'm unable to eat, precisely *when* I eat does matter. As with many things in life, but especially for meals and me, timing is everything.

Laughing Matters²

Snowshoeing in the northern New Mexico mountains near Angel Fire, Tom and I have the forest to ourselves. The deep, fresh snow glistens in the bright morning sunshine streaming through the trees. Crisp, cold mountain air startles our lungs and chills our exposed faces. Other than our voices and sometimes labored breathing, the only sound is the rhythmic crunch of the snow beneath our feet.

Breaking trail in deep, new snow requires exertion. We pause from time to time to catch our breath. Tom, a relatively new friend, was unaware that I had Parkinson's disease until I suddenly interrupt our trek, pull a well-stocked pill case from my pocket, and announce, "I need to take a short break for some 'performance-enhancing drugs'."

Seeing my stash, he says, "Boy, you weren't kidding, were you?"

As I down the pills, I offer a brief explanation of my Parkinson's-driven drug dependency. I conclude with a mock-serious declaration.

"With all the drugs I take, I'm something of a walking chemistry experiment."

Since we are already on snowshoes, I can't resist another of my often-repeated pretenses. "I don't know if I've mentioned this, but I've got my first decree planned for when I'm running the universe."

"When you're running the universe? And what exactly will your decree be?"

"Well, everyone will be required to wear snowshoes all the time. I'm not any clumsier on snowshoes than anyone else. So, the way I've got it figured, snowshoes will be the great equalizer. Problem solved!"

Parkinson's disease is, of course, no laughing matter. There's nothing funny about the tortured existence of many in my cohort. Yet, I've always found a sense of humor helpful in managing the inevitable strains that punctuate our lives. And so it is with Parkinson's. Some experiences just plain strike me funny. In addition, I have some stock one-liners calculated to ease discomfort, both for me and for concerned observers of my struggles. I can't resist repeating them.

There are the unpredicted episodes like the salsa dance lessons Dianne advocated as recreational physical therapy. At the conclusion of our group lesson, I'm paired with a young woman dance partner. She and I have never met. I feel a bit awkward holding this stranger in a close dance embrace. I wonder about her possible discomfort. For starters, I'm much older than she, and I'm not likely to be as graceful as many of the other dancers.

With her right arm raised to meet my left, the music begins. Simultaneously, a mild parkinsonian tremor begins in my elevated left hand. The woman looks at my hand, then looks at me. She looks again at my hand, glances over her right shoulder, and then looks back at me.

"Who are you waving at?" she says, oblivious that this is a symptom of disease. I don't want her to feel embarrassed by her naïveté, so I suppress my urge to laugh and withhold the fact that this is a symptom of Parkinson's disease.

"Oh, sometimes my hand just shakes," I say.

Every now and then I devise a grand strategy for a kind of first-strike solution to my balance and coordination problems. This sometimes yields absurd results. Taos Ski Valley's highly acclaimed "ski week" was one such episode.

The previous winter season, my skiing had become raggedly unsafe. This was underscored on my final run of the day down to the base area. The trail was narrow, sometimes steep, and bordered a tree-lined and partially frozen creek. My balance and coordination had become so compromised that

I took the kind of fall my grandchildren refer to as a yard sale. In a skiing yard sale, you strike the ground with such intensity that your gear is strewn haphazardly about the slope. My skis had come off, my goggles were disconnected from my helmet, and my ski poles were ripped from my hands. It was a bona fide yard sale, indeed.

For the uninitiated, Taos ski week offers a daily, weeklong, high-quality series of small-group ski lessons. With unsubstantiated optimism, I was convinced that my new ski boots and expert instruction would solve my neurologically based skiing problems.

The week begins with a ski-off. Each student in succession skis a short, steep area, past an array of instructors positioned at regular intervals along the slope. The teachers' trained eyes evaluate each skier's ability and assign the student to a class level.

Adrenaline building, my turn comes. I shoot down the mountain past the entire complement of instructors, make a single turn, and stop. The head instructor shouts out a number designating the class level at which he has judged my ability. His assessment is shockingly above where I believe myself to be. Visions of orthopedic-surgery hell dominate my thoughts.

"Thanks for the compliment, but that's really far above my level," I say.

"I *know* where you fit," he responds.

"With all due respect, I'm sure I'm not at the level you've assigned."

"Look, I watched you. You skied straight down the mountain and made a single turn. You're a very aggressive skier."

"I'm afraid you weren't really seeing what you think you were seeing," I counter.

"I've been teaching skiing for decades, with hundreds of skiers. I *know* where you belong."

"But what you were watching was someone 'shopping' for a turn. It's not that I didn't want to turn. I couldn't turn. I have a neurological disorder," I plead.

He finally relents and puts me at a lower level than he'd originally assigned. It's still above the level at which I belong. Over the next couple of days, I further demote myself and finally drop out of the class.

Having survived my ski-school escapade physically intact, I found a far less life-threatening laugh-inducing situation during a visit with my neurologist, Dr. Jill. Quarterly visits with Jill are a fact of my life. Dianne accompanies me, ready to rat me out should I fail to respond to the doctor's questions with what she deems the absolute truth.

Among the medicines I take, one lists compulsive behavior as a potential side effect. Partway into my visit, Dr. Jill inquires, "Have you had any compulsive behavior?"

"Well, I probably eat too much, but that's about it," I answer.

Dr. Jill detects a dissenting expression on Dianne's face.

"You disagree?" she asks Dianne.

"He's compulsively spending money," she declares.

Dr. Jill appears concerned.

"Is it serious, like driving you to the point of bankruptcy?"

"Well, no," Dianne answers.

Dr. Jill turns her attention back to me. "What exactly are you spending money on?"

"Rubber duckies," I say. "It's part of my campaign to make the world a kinder and gentler place. It's impossible for someone not to smile when you hand one to them. I've bought several dozen of them."

"And how much do these rubber duckies cost?"

"Oh, about a buck each."

Dr. Jill pauses and sits back in her chair. She looks at Dianne. Then she looks back at me.

"Look, folks, I'm a neurologist. I don't *do* marriage counseling. I'm afraid you'll just have to work this one out on your own."

Some, like my friend Dirk, share my appreciation of life's absurdity. Dirk had never been snowshoeing, and I agreed to introduce him to it. He is the rare survivor of a near 95 percent fatal heart condition. Given that fact, he is required to keep his heart rate below a certain level. So, having chosen what I believe to be a gentle introductory location, we proceed along a trail not far from our Taos home. It's a mild and sunny winter day. There's virtually no one around save us.

Midway into our trek, we rest on a large fallen tree trunk. I've been assuring Dirk, "Just up ahead, there's a meadow we can cut across. It'll significantly shorten our trek." Each time we've paused to rest over the preceding half-hour, I've confidently asserted that the cutoff would be "just another few minutes ... around the bend ... over the next rise." But despite my assurances, we are not yet there.

As we sit on a fallen log, I offer Dirk an energy bar. "Don't you think we should save it for when it gets dark?" he says. "And just think about this. Suppose one of us gets hurt. You can't run and I shouldn't. Who goes for help?" Fifty-five-year-old Dirk loves to tell people, "This 70-year-old man took me snowshoeing and tried to kill me."

Though I wish it were otherwise, having Parkinson's doesn't immunize you against having another disease. So, Parkinson's notwithstanding, I'm not shocked when the pain in my foot turns out be a stress fracture. I am, however, disappointed that at

the very start of the winter outdoor recreation season, there will be no skiing or snowshoeing for me.
For weeks, I've been making plans with friends, and
had already been snowshoeing and skiing with
Dianne. The task now at hand involves figuring out
what I can do for exercise while wearing the rigid
boot prescribed by my podiatrist.

I begin experimenting with various exercise
devices at our local spa, but the still unseasonably
warm and sunny early-December afternoons make a
golfing attempt the most attractive possibility.

"Wanna try nine holes with me?" I ask Dianne.

"Will you be able to play with the boot on?" she
asks.

"We'll find out. I won't be able to walk the course
with it on. I'll ride. If you're up for it, we'll give it a
try."

"OK, then," she responds. At noon the very next
day we're on the first tee. To my surprise and delight,
boot and all, my first drive is nice and straight — and
about 180 yards — as far as I ever hit the ball. And
that's the way it goes for most of the round. There
are, however, a couple of noteworthy exceptions.
Surprisingly, I manage drives of 200 and 230 yards
on two of the holes. Both drives are significantly
farther than I've ever hit. In addition, the 230-yard
drive was straight down the middle of the fairway
on the course's toughest hole.

Back home, I'm still brimming with pride as I unload our golf clubs. Lee, a friend and an excellent golfer, notices my activity.

"Been out on the course?" he inquires.

"Yeah, and I played better in the boot," I respond. "Wearing it is my new game-improvement strategy. When my foot is healed, I'm going to keep golfing in the boot. The way I've got it figured, if I get a boot for the other foot, I'm about ready to join the pro tour!"

Call it comic relief, whistling past the graveyard, or some perverse preoccupation with patent absurdities. In the end, there is no humor in Parkinson's disease. No matter how energetically I may search, it's still not a laughing matter. But it sure beats sitting around in a pool of self-pity. Compared to that, I guess I'll go for the cheap laugh any day.

---

2) An earlier version of this essay appeared in R.J. Silver, *Tributes & Tirades: Taos Life and American Politics*, Nighthawk Press, 2013, pp. 37-41.

A Peak Experience

The whole outing seemed charged with absurdity. A couple of nights earlier, I could barely navigate the short distances between Don and Debbie's dining room, their front door, and their driveway. Yet, here the four of us are, driving up the steep, bumpy, winding dirt road above Taos Ski Valley's base area. We are en route to the Williams Lake trailhead and possibly to the summit of Wheeler Peak, New Mexico's highest point at 13,161 feet. Dianne and Don are committed to reaching the summit. Debbie has signed on for the much more modest goal of Williams Lake. I'm up in the air as to how far past Williams Lake I would or could go. In earlier less Parkinson's-impacted times, I had never reached Wheeler's summit. Why would I think I could hike it a decade after being diagnosed?

It's near 8 a.m. on a beautiful mid-September morning as we pull into the trailhead parking area. It's a bit later than ideal starting time, given the always unpredictable summit weather, but it's still clear and cool. Though I've been awake since 3 a.m., I feel energized by the cool mountain air. Ready to get on up the trail, I quickly gather my equipment and down a dose of Stalevo, my performance-enhancing drug of the moment.

Gotta make sure to keep the medicine schedule in focus. All depends on how well it works today. May have to tinker with it.

Reluctant to stand around in the chill mountain morning, I lead out at an unsustainable clip.

"I'm not going to be able to keep up this pace for long," Don exclaims.

"No worries. I won't either. You'll probably see me slow down to a near crawl before too long," I respond.

I'm clipping along now, but I may crash and burn at some point.

Deep in conversation, Dianne and Debbie are proceeding far more slowly. Don and I are soon much farther up the trail.

As we walk and talk, a reflection billows within me. We'd been to a literary event the previous evening. Larry, a doctor-writer friend, read a piece regarding his struggle to keep hiking his beloved New Mexico mountains despite Parkinson's disease. He was unaware of my plans to hike here this morning. Yet, as we exited the event, he stopped me to tell me that he'd read this particular piece especially for me. During the short drive home, his words remained with me.

Was this oblique encouragement to follow his lead? Am I obliged to do anything he can do? Did I, too, bear a near-moral obligation to openly and fully live life, Parkinson's notwithstanding?

Continuing up the trail, my friend Dirk is also in my thoughts. He was due back in Taos following an extremely risky open-heart surgery — his second. Incredibly, he came through this latest surgery in spectacular fashion and is homeward bound some ten days post-op. Dirk had stared down the prospect of his own demise. As I hike, I can't help feeling both inspired and daunted by the determined courage of my friends.

See how I feel when we reach the Wheeler Peak cut-off. Not sure how far I can go. No commitment to summit. Just turn back, if necessary. Debbie's not going to the summit anyway.

As we pick our way up the rocky logging road that leads to the Wheeler Peak Wilderness entry point, Don and I talk about the greater pleasure of traversing this initial part of the trail in winter on snowshoes when the deep fresh snow cushions the rock-strewn surface. Though the road is studded with large rocks, they are less of a barrier for me than one might think.

"I actually find it easier on this rocky part than I would if the path were really smooth. It's puzzling. It's as if rocks provide some sort of fixed visual cue for each footstep," I speculate.

And so we proceed on up the trail to our Williams Lake way point. From time to time, Don and I pause to let the women catch up. We then resume our trek, reaching the Wheeler Peak trail intersection in an hour and a half. Now for the tough part.

Pausing briefly at this decision point, we restate our earlier commitments. Dianne and Don are still all in for the summit. I'll keep going and see how I feel. Debbie, too, will continue up the trail as far as she's able. For the time being, we're all on board. I again take the lead, into a deeply forested part of the trail. I'm still feeling energetic. My gait is acceptably fluid. My pharmaceutical supplements are still at work.

Now the uncertain part. Gained about a thousand feet. Another 2,000 feet to the summit. Probably going to be another three hours or so of climbing. Then, no choice but hike back down.

Hiking the shaded forest is a joy. Though we sometimes encounter steep sections, the cool quiet of the thick forest, combined with relaxed conversation, renders our trek temporarily pleasurable. Along the way, we encounter a female trainer from our fitness center. Stephanie had coincidentally been involved in Don's cardiac rehabilitation program some years earlier.

Before long, we emerge from the forest above timberline. On the now-unprotected trail, we will be subject to alternating periods of strong, warming sun and breezy, cooling cloudiness. In the worst case, we could be at risk, should the good weather suddenly morph into one of the area's frequent thunderstorms. That would confront us with potentially grave danger, forcing us to hurry back down the mountain, at least to the relative protection of the forest. In my case, a quick descent would likely be an oxymoron. Fortunately, the weather appears good and holding.

The trail's texture varies widely. Sometimes the grade is particularly steep; at other times, relatively gentle. Occasionally, the surface is smooth and sandy. Then there are long sections of loose, rocky scree, where footing can be precarious. At still other points, the trail offers stair-step-like protrusions. Again, these rocky sections are easier for me to negotiate than the smooth sections preferred by most others.

Don and I continue our routine, pausing from time to time to allow Dianne and Debbie to rejoin us. It's now clear that Debbie is not going to make it to the summit. Dianne and Don are still determined to reach the top. I'm still unsure how far my medicine will carry me. Though I'm on a three-hour cycle, I shorten the interval to two hours and take the next dose. I hike along at Debbie's pace and encourage the others to proceed as they wish.

For the next hour and a half or so, we fall into a parallel pattern. I maintain a position close behind Debbie, waiting with her as she recovers from the exertion. I encourage her while trying not to push her beyond her limit; but she's clearly tiring.

"I'm sorry to slow you down," she repeats whenever she stops to rest.

"No problem. Who knows how far I'll get. May not get any further than you," is my repetitive refrain.

As we ascend further, we encounter more loose scree. The temperature has dropped, but there doesn't seem to be any storm danger. Once we reach 12,000 feet, I begin to call out each additional hundred-foot altitude gain. At 12,500 feet, Debbie has had enough. She declares her intention to head back down. After checking to make sure she feels safe on her own, I hand her my car keys. "You'll have a more comfortable place to hang out while you wait for us," I tell her.

My balance and coordination seem to be holding with 500 to 600 feet of elevation gain yet to go. Now on my own, I pick up the pace. The climbing demands more effort in the ever-thinning air. The broad stretches of scree require full focus.

At last, nearing a saddle-like ridge, a tall, broad rock cairn comes into view. I'm hoping this marks the summit. But no; I've still got another couple hundred feet of elevation to climb. I now have a growing headache from high-altitude exertion. Gazing up the remaining stretch of trail, I pause to pee, catch my breath, and marshal my resolve.

Just a bit further. Push yourself. You can make it.

Forcing my body onward, I see Don coming toward me. "Can I help you the rest of the way?" he offers.

"No. I think I can make it from here," I respond. "But thanks for the company."

The steep, rocky ridge now underfoot is the final challenge. Its jagged protrusions again feel a bit like stairsteps.

I can do this. Just keep going.

As I near the summit, Dianne captures my final steps with her iPhone camera. I'm elated, surprised, and exhausted. Who would have thought it? Now, all I need to worry about is the trek back down. Hey, no choice. I'll have to keep going, even though the day's hike will turn out to be eight hours up and back.

Hearing of this surprising and unlikely excursion, friends and acquaintances have asked, "How did you do it?" Mostly, my response is, "I don't really know." I do, however, have a guess. I believe it all starts with the example of courageous determination shown by my friends, Larry and Dirk. Then there is my wife Dianne's constant encouragement to remain fully physically active. Finally, on this particular day, there was the gentle support of our friends and hiking companions, Don and Debbie. While the medication and its management are vital, necessary conditions, ultimately, the people who lead, encourage, and support are equally important.

Though the eight-hour slog left me drained and depleted, I felt a sense of accomplishment in doing it. This is not something that someone with Parkinson's disease is ever expected to do. "I'm never doing this again!" I declare.

Yet, some nine months later, I'm at it again, preparing for another try at the Wheeler Peak summit. An old saying comes to mind: "There's nothing to be learned from the second kick of a mule!"

So, what am I doing here?

I've joked with friends that my reversal must make me a man of my most recent word. However, two unforeseen developments induce me to violate my pledge. One is a national effort to raise funds for Parkinson's research. One million dollars was pledged for the cause through a succession of athletic challenges (climbing, biking, running) in each of the United States. In New Mexico, the event coincidentally and serendipitously is a group assault on Wheeler Peak. The other development is that my dear and generous friend, Lucy, has taken it upon herself to organize a local team named in my honor. With both a national and a very personal home effort in place, how could I decline to play my part in it?

Having now summited for the second time, I've again vowed, "never again!" This time, I really mean it. Unless, of course, my friends find some other means to make a liar of me.

With a Nod to Narcissism and a Dash of Denial

"You, take the front wheels. And you, lift with the grips on the back of the chair. On my signal, lift me up the stairs and roll me forward through the doorway."

"Kenneth" calmly and confidently commanded these surprised, apparently able-bodied bystanders. He was like a ship's captain issuing orders to his crew. He was undaunted by the fact that he had never met the people he was pressing into service and had no authority to direct their actions.

I first encountered Kenneth at a long-ago dinner with a small group of Houston colleagues. A wheelchair-bound paraplegic and professional acquaintance, he had lost both legs early in life in a catastrophic automobile accident. Though physically challenged, he was a husband and parent, had an active social life, traveled widely, and pursued a busy career in psychology. One key to his mobility seemed to rest with his improvised sense of enti-tlement. He lacked compunction regarding drawing upon the physical capacities of others whenever and wherever his need might arise. I marveled at the ease with which he commandeered the services of any and all around him. It seemed a sort of "adaptive narcissism."

Fast forward to my own, then unforeseen, mobility challenges, courtesy of Parkinson's disease. Though I'm not without legs, mine sometimes seem as useless as if they were Kenneth's missing limbs. A recent evening activity contrasts with his easy comfort appropriating the assistance of others.

Following attendance at a couple of art-gallery opening receptions, Dianne and I are bound for a quiet dinner at a favorite restaurant. Throughout the reception, my body has not been responding to the medications that usually allow for relatively normal-appearing mobility. This particular evening, though I'm present at the gallery's cocktail party, I remain relatively fixed in place. It's as if I am an eddy-establishing boulder in the flow of people streaming past me. I shuffle my feet laboriously to change position when I must. All the while, I try desperately to not call attention to myself and my frozen state.

As the time for our dinner reservation draws near, it's clear that my medication is just not going to work well. I'd hoped to execute a stealthy exit from the gallery, but that's not in the cards this evening. To the contrary, an assortment of friends, acquaintances, and total strangers take increasing notice of my fixed stance and posture. At a time like this, I find myself wishing I could be invisible. I'd like to muddle through as best I can without an audience. If I'm dividing my attention between putting one foot in front of the other and being preoccupied with how others may be reacting to my obvious impairment, it magnifies the difficulty of getting out the door.

But why should I care that others take note of my condition? It's not as if I hide the fact of this disease. To the contrary, I'm quite open about having it. Witness the fact of my choosing to write about it. I suspect that the explanation resides in some as-yet-unfinished personal history.

As an adult, I probably would not be thought to lack self-confidence. Yet that's precisely who and how I was as a youngster: shy, anxious, insecure. The Parkinson's physical ineptness that becomes obvious to others when I hit an immobility period seems to rekindle feelings of shame that were all too common in my early life. It's as if, once again, I'm not the person I'm supposed to be — one whose body is strong, graceful, and reliable. Parkinson's symptoms seem to revive vestiges of that ancient childhood anguish.

This brings me back to Kenneth and what I have always thought of as his display of a kind of adaptive narcissism. While people usually think of narcissism in uniformly negative terms, a small amount of it can be a useful thing. Doing anything truly challenging in life requires a little bit of narcissism. When I reflect, for example, on the self-confidence that a surgeon must possess, holding the power of life or death in his or her hands, sticking a scalpel into another human being's body, I'm happy for the doctor to be a bit narcissistic (i.e., self-assured). I am reminded of the famous words of Rabbi Hillel: "If I am not for myself, then who will be for me?" Those in my Parkinson's cohort probably serve themselves best by being at least a bit adaptively narcissistic.

Just as narcissism is usually thought of as pathological, denial — a well-known psychological defense mechanism — is typically considered an especially maladaptive device. Among the more primitive and ultimately ineffective of psychological defense mechanisms, it is the functional equivalent of closing one's eyes to reality and being temporarily blind to what may provoke anxiety. While it may have some limited, short-term utility, it's a strategy inevitably doomed to failure. Nevertheless, I have found it useful to selectively employ a philosophy based on denial in managing the predictable losses of function inherent in Parkinson's disease. I've labeled this approach "adaptive denial."

Running was the first of my regular recreational activities that I fully relinquished. Although I hadn't discovered the pleasure of running until I'd reached my early forties, I was hooked on it for decades. Now that I'm sometimes profoundly immobile, I feel deep nostalgia for earlier fleet-footed times that I took for granted.

Like most runners, I have fond memories of special times and places to which my once-energized legs transported me. There was the spring Saturday-morning jog among the heroic monuments of Washington, D.C., highlighted by a run up the steps of the Lincoln Memorial. A momentary Sylvester Stallone mimic, arms raised in triumph, I could almost hear the "Rocky" theme music in the background. There were the years of charity fun runs, like Austin's Capitol 10K spring running carnival and San Francisco's unmatched Bay to Breakers annual jogging circus, which stretched from San Francisco Bay up and across the hills of the city to the Pacific Ocean shore. There were the regular Saturday-morning jogs with friends along Austin's magnificent Town Lake, the place where I met my Dianne.

But best of all was the impromptu run through the Tuscan countryside with my friend Mike. Dianne and I, along with three other couples, had rented a farmhouse 10 kilometers south of Sienna, an ancient walled Italian city. One particularly beautiful spring morning during our stay, Mike and I impulsively pulled on our running shoes and headed out into the countryside. We had confidently announced our intention to return shortly and join the group's touring plan for the day. Setting out from the farmhouse, though completely unfamiliar with the area, we had neither care nor concern as to where we were headed or how we would get there. The weather was just too perfect, the countryside too beautiful, the moment too magical.

The rolling hills and serene, towering Cypress trees bordering the rural road we were traveling urged us ever onward, further and further from our starting point. It was a siren song that we were powerless to resist, inexorably encouraging our advance toward Sienna. We were on an Italian-tinged runners' high, totally lost in the moment, lacking any sense of time, distance — or our commitment to our friends. Though subsequently scolded for our protracted absence, we were neither contrite nor repentant. The others simply didn't understand. We had serendipitously been to the runner's promised land. The disapproval of spouses and friends couldn't compete with that.

The progression of Parkinson's disease ended my recreational running. Though ungainly, I am in fact capable of running; yet Parkinson's renders my gait so abnormal that I bruise the metatarsals in my feet when I do. The resulting foot pain makes it not worth the cost.

As I've often declared, I am determined to play the hand I've been dealt and live the life before me in full. It's often a struggle to continue with the pleasures and pastimes that have long been parts of my life. I persist in recreational athletic activities and exercise, though slower, clumsier, and without grace. I have refused to relinquish any of these pursuits unless and until there are incontrovertible data demanding that I quit. Thus far, jogging is the one activity that I have totally abandoned. In time, skiing, tennis, golfing, hiking, and biking will doubtless be beyond my grasp. Nevertheless, I intend to continue until there is clear evidence of risk. Primitive though it may be, this strategy of selective denial has been adaptive for me.

Just Like Tango

"No more backward walking!" was Dr. Jill's decree. I'd shared with her my curious and counterintuitive experience of sometimes being able to walk backward when I'm unable to walk forward. Out of concern for the danger inherent in being unable to see where I'm going, she directed me to eliminate this from my array of coping strategies. While I deeply appreciate, value, and trust her professional judgment, sometimes ya gotta do what ya gotta do.

And so it was, one bright, sunny fall afternoon.

Dianne and I are driving with our dog, Shadow, to Taos's Kit Carson Park. While we much prefer to walk this short distance, I have some premonition regarding the reliability of my walking. We are bound for the Wool Festival, a carnivalesque annual happening where fiber artists exhibit their latest offerings. Though the event draws a large crowd, my disabled-parking permit scores a close-in parking space.

We exit my car and make our way across the parking lot to a large, grassy open space. Dozens of white, cabana-like booths line the perimeter of this broad, unfenced lawn. Wandering among the booths, we pause to examine the artisans' wares and to chat with friends and acquaintances we encounter. We eventually reach the booth of our friends Fred and Daryl. We are fans of Fred's Southwestern-themed woven wool rugs. We had previously commissioned one of his creations that now softens the stone entry to our home.

Our other connection to this couple is an unlikely one. Both Fred and his wife, Daryl, are avid tango dancers. Over several years, they have been fellow students and dance partners in various dance classes.

The flow of potential rug buyers has slowed a bit, and Fred and Daryl are able to chat with us. After 15 minutes, Dianne is ready to move on; there's a baby llama exhibit area 50 to 100 yards away. She is confident that Shadow will enjoy seeing it. As for me, my balance and coordination have become more uncertain as we stand and visit with Fred and Daryl. A familiar disappointing sensation has crept back into my legs, which now feel increasingly leaden. So I beg off on this small side trip.

"Not walking so well?" asks Dianne.

"I'm not. I think I'll just hang out around here. You go on and see the animals. I might sit down over by that tent." I gesture in the direction of a large temporary shelter in the middle of the grassy area.

"Well, all right, if you're sure you'll be OK," she replies.

"I'll be OK."

Dianne heads off. Daryl appears increasingly concerned. Having danced with me in the past, she is aware of my mobility struggles.

"Can I help?" she inquires.

"Thanks, but no, you can't," I respond. "But I can probably walk backward. Watch." Still facing Daryl, my back generally oriented in the direction of Dianne's departure, I slowly extend my right leg backward. Then I tentatively execute a long, slow, backward stride with my left leg. Then another, and another.

"It's like tango!" Daryl exclaims. "Long backward strides."

She's now got a big grin on her face, as she, too, takes a few backward strides across the grass. It's as if we've discovered a new game or a new tango venue. Her worried look evaporates.

Dianne has now returned.

"Still not walking so well?" she asks.

"No, not yet," I reply.

"Well, what should we do? Should I go back to the car and get your wheels?"

"No. There's no way I'll be able to make the

thing roll on this thick grass. Tell you what. I know Jill doesn't want me walking backward, but I'm out of options. So, let's do this. I'll walk backward to the car, while you guide me so I don't run into anything."

Dianne and I lock arms. She is temporarily my eyes. Shadow takes up a position on Dianne's other side. Heeling more scrupulously than ever, he seems to know it's game on! He does not strain at his lead, and faithfully matches our uncommonly slow pace. We commence our odd trio walk.

Partnering in this strange dance requires more guidance for Dianne than for Shadow. It's not that different from our recreational dancing. Dianne is not a born follower, and yet I need her to adjust to my lead as far as pace and length of stride. "Let me step back first, with as long a stride as I can. You try to match what I do."

"OK, I'll try," she says.

Shortly, she is matching my movements, and we are making progress toward the parking area some hundred yards away.

As we proceed, people we pass appear puzzled by our antics. Their stares, sidelong glances, and smiles suggest that they don't know what to make of us. Are we playing some kind of game? Clowning around? Seeking attention? The silent speculation of onlookers is finally ended by a couple heading in the same direction.

"You must really be needing a challenge," the man conjectures.

"No," I answer. "I've got Parkinson's disease. Sometimes I just walk better backward."

"Well, good luck. God bless you," he says.

Dianne, Shadow, and I are now crossing the roadway entrance to the park. A woman calls out to Dianne.

"Have you got him in a hammer lock?"

Almost back at my car, we smile, but we neither reply nor break stride, now that we've got a bit of momentum going. Safely in the car, we three collaborators share a tacit understanding that no great disservice to my medical care will be done in not advising Dr. Jill of my violation of her "no backward walking" edict. Dianne is a co-conspirator. So, for once, she's probably not going to rat me out. But I'm not betting on it.

The Coming Crises

It's four a.m. Time to start the new day's meds. I swallow the prescribed handful of pills. Anticipating the now-routine one-hour delay for the drugs to restore some semblance of mobility, Dianne and I have scheduled a spinning class for six. I expect to be moving by five and ready to go as planned well before the class start time. But this morning things are not going the way I'd assumed. An hour has elapsed, and I'm still barely able to move. I'm filled with dread, alarm, and creeping despair. I've suddenly plunged over an emotional cliff.

The drugs aren't working! Is this the end of the line? Has my optimistic bravado now been reduced to a self-mocking charade? Maybe it's just some transient, unexplainable anomaly. Will Dr. Jill be able to rescue me yet again? Has the prophesied grim existence finally come to pass? Have I deluded myself into thinking that I could somehow avoid this rendezvous with my destiny? How grandiose!

It seems reasonable for me to be thinking along these lines, since a similar scenario unfolded just yesterday. That day began with a three-hour wait for the morning medicine to bring reasonable movement. I'd persuaded myself that my metabolism was probably just a bit off and that's what was causing my problems. I had a strangely unsettled feeling in my gut. That, I decided, must be the explanation. Given the vicissitudes of my neurotransmission, all theories seem initially plausible.

But today brings a rerun of the home horror movie that premiered yesterday. My rationalizations no longer allay my escalating anxiety. Parkinson's relentless assault is overpowering my pharmaceuticals' capacity to maintain my confidence. This is the nature of the disease's progression. I'm always playing catch-up.

Since the standard therapy protocol is to try to get by with as little mobility-enabling medicine as possible for as long as possible, I'm constantly at risk for the medication's sudden failure and the full-blown return of immobilizing symptoms. It's an ongoing balancing act. I dare not increase the medication dosage too soon or I run the risk of living beyond the drugs' ability to manage my symptoms. Additionally, too much medicine will guarantee an increase in disconcerting dyskinesia, the random, uncoordinated, involuntary motor flurries that one sees in someone like actor Michael J. Fox. So, I must wait until my symptoms are no longer effectively controlled at the current medication level before a dosage increase is prudent.

My status regarding our scheduled morning exercise class is uncertain. Dianne seems in a quandary regarding my wishes. Parkinson's most direct impact is upon me. Yet in refusing to grant neutral, noncombatant status to those who love or care for me, it distorts Dianne's life, too. I'm determined to resist its damage to others in my life and do all I can to limit its impact on this woman I love.

"Should I wait?" she asks.

"Why don't you get going. I'll be along as soon as possible."

"Do you want me to save a bike for you?" she asks.

"That would be great. I'll be there when I can."

She complies with my urging and heads for her car. Several minutes later, I make my way to my car. I twist my body into the driver's seat, back the car out of the garage and head off through the predawn darkness. I hope my medicine will be working in time for class.

As I guide my car into the parking space closest to the spa entry, it's still unclear if I'll be able to manage the 20-foot distance to the building's interior. I open the car door and hoist myself through its ample opening. Through a succession of improvised handholds, I gradually make my way along the driver's side of the car to the tailgate. Will I be able to negotiate the free space to the building's entry? After about 15 minutes of effort, the answer is clearly "no." This is not to be my morning. Disappointed, I reverse direction and inch my way back to the mechanized mobility of my car. Several minutes after arriving back home, my medicine is again working. But it's too late for the plans I'd made.

Over the next couple of days, I feel like I'm at war with both Parkinson's and myself. I obsess over whether this could in fact be some strange anomaly that I can ride out or if I need to call Dr. Jill. I desperately don't want to sound a false alarm. I don't want to be needlessly needy. But the pattern seems to be with me for keeps. I struggle through days of increased imprisonment in my own body. The three-hour delay before my morning pharmaceutical cocktail finally takes effect is the new norm. Even then, I only get some six hours of mobility for the entire day.

It's late Friday afternoon when I finally concede the reality of my new reality.

"It's not getting any better," I tell Dianne.

As if she didn't already know this.

"I'm gonna call Jill."

"Good," she says.

With that, I'm released from the irrational fantasy that I can simply will my impaired neurological system to do as I wish. This mind-set is the downside of my determination to be no more dependent than I must be. It's always a tough call for me to ask for help. I telephone Dr. Jill.

Given my delay in contacting her, the weekend has already begun. Nevertheless, Jill returns my call within the half-hour. I relate the facts of my diminished response to the current drug regimen and convey my regret at having intruded into her weekend. She listens patiently, unemotionally, quietly. The drama is all within *me*. She is matter-of-fact in her analysis.

"We want to keep you on the three-hour schedule that you're on, so let's increase the Stalevo from 75mg to 100mg. Where do you get your medication? I'll send an electronic prescription for the increased dose."

"Thanks so much," I reply. It's Express Scrips mail order. Thanks for your help."

As Dr. Jill extends this lifeline, Dianne waits beside me listening to every word of my telephone exchange. She has a flurry of questions.

"Jill is increasing your dose from 75 to 100? Which of the medicines is she changing? What are you going to do until the new pills get here?"

"She's increasing the Stalevo. I've got some leftover 50s I've hoarded from an earlier prescription. I'll cannibalize them until the new 100s arrive."

Dianne has still more questions.

"Is it OK to do that? Will they still work? Have you got enough to last you?"

Assuming my plan would be frowned upon by most pharmacists and physicians, I sidestep Dianne's question regarding the legitimacy of getting by with out-of-date, leftover pills.

"I'll check with the pharmacy regarding the old pills' potency. I'm pretty sure I can stretch them out until the new ones get here."

To resolve my current medication crash, I gladly substitute the increased dosage Dr. Jill has prescribed. In the ensuing 48 hours, my restored mobility confirms that she has rescued me yet again. I'm back to my normal level of movement and optimism. If only this pharmaceutical lifeline could be deployed without so much angst on my part. When the bottom drops out next time, and there will be a next time, I wish I could be unequivocally confident that Jill will ably come to my rescue yet again.

Weeks later, Jill provides precisely the reassurance I seek. At 10 o'clock, Dianne and I are Jill's first appointment on this lovely spring morning. Jill is dressed as usual in her decidedly nonmedical athletic clothing. She appears rested and relaxed as she greets us.

During the two-and-a-half-hour drive to Jill's office, Dianne had asked, "What questions do you have for Jill?"

"I'd like her advice on how I might better manage the next time the medicine stops working," I'd replied. The long drive had given me time to think this over. I'm now seated in Jill's office. Here's my opening.

"I'm glad to see that you're not in your office any earlier than this. I feel kind of protective of you. It's a matter of self-interest," I announce.

Jill smiles as she deflects my playful role reversal. She moves on to the medical business at hand. Following her review of my mishaps and medications since my last visit and her examination of my muscle rigidity, reflexes, posture, and gait, I have a chance to raise the question I've been pondering.

"The next time the medicine stops being effective, is there some way I can handle it more smoothly?" I ask.

Either by dint of her extensive experience, or because of her keen sensitivity, Jill immediately penetrates the heart of the disabling anxiety that the medication's periodic failure evokes in me.

"The disease will progress gradually. It's not suddenly going to get dramatically worse. We'll be able to adjust the medication to deal with it. I've done that with other patients for decades. I'll be doing the same with you. You'll be a member of the club whose members have been doing well for a long time."

The yearned-for reassurance is right on target. Jill's gotten precisely to my core concern. I need hear no more. I leave her office confident that my next crash will be less traumatic. With Jill and Dianne in my corner, I feel much more secure.

I'm reinvigorated as we head for home. It is indeed a beautiful spring day. The gratitude I feel toward my angel of medical mercy is unbounded. Weeks ago, Jill restored my mobility. Now, she's shored up my confidence. For me, it just doesn't get much better than this.

Movin' On

It's as predictable as it could be. Any time I set foot in a courtroom, one or more determined attorneys will do their very best to portray me to a judge or a jury as a liar, a fool, or worse. It comes with the expert-witness territory of forensic-psychology practice. Rarely personal, it's just business — the business of whichever attorney's case might be harmed by the judgment I've rendered. That person's job is to discredit me and the professional opinion I hold. It's the context in which I've worked for decades. But it makes me especially alert to any display of my Parkinson's symptoms.

The best trial lawyers I've known speak of court proceedings as theater. Appearance and perception matter. On the witness stand, one must look, sound, and act the part played. In this case, it is the role of the honest broker of expert knowledge. Given my progressing Parkinson's disease, I'm mindful that a judge or jury might misconstrue an errant tremor or compromised mobility as anxiety, uncertainty, or discomfort with the court proceeding. A hostile attorney might even willfully misrepresent it as such. I imagine a future scenario unfolding something like this:

ATTORNEY HOSTILE: Dr. Silver, I'm Attorney Hostile. I have a few questions I'd like to ask regarding the testimony you've just given. My opposing counsel, Attorney Friendly, asked you to specify the degree of medical certainty that you assigned to the opinion you offered in your testimony. I believe you testified that you had a high degree of medical certainty regarding your opinion about my client. Is that correct?

ME: That's correct.

MR. HOSTILE: Now, in forming your opinion, you spent many hours conducting an IME [independent medical examination] of my client. Is that correct?

ME: It is.

MR. HOSTILE: Is that a yes or a no, Doctor?

ME: It's a yes. I spent a full day conducting the IME.

MR. HOSTILE: If you would answer my questions with a simple yes or no, I would appreciate it.

ME: OK, but some questions don't lend themselves to simple yes or no answers.

MR. HOSTILE: Dr. Silver, let's just cross that bridge when we come to it, if you don't mind. OK?

ME: OK.

MR. HOSTILE: Can we return, then, to the IME you conducted?

ME: Sure.

MR. HOSTILE: My understanding is that your IME involved several evaluation techniques and tests. Is that correct?

ME: Yes. That's correct.

MR. HOSTILE: And among those evaluation methods were some psychological tests and something called a "mental status exam?" Is that correct?

ME: Yes, that is correct.

MR. HOSTILE: You also conducted a several-hours-long interview of my client. Do I have that right?

ME: Yes. That's right.

MR. HOSTILE: Dr. Silver, when you do a forensic psychology interview, I understand that you ask a number of questions. Is it also correct that you don't just listen to the content of the interviewee's answers, but that you also take note of what you call "behavioral observations?"

ME: That's correct. Yes.

MR. HOSTILE: So, when you testified that my client showed signs of "psy-cho-mo-tor retardation," am I pronouncing this right?

ME: Psychomotor retardation is the pronunciation.

MR. HOSTILE: Is this something that you would classify as a "behavioral observation?"

ME: Is *what* something I would classify as a "behavioral observation?"

MR. HOSTILE: I'm sorry. Perhaps my question was not clear. Is psychomotor retardation something you would classify as a "behavioral observation?"

ME: Well, actually, psychomotor retardation would be the conceptualization or interpretation given to some observed actual behaviors.

MR. HOSTILE: Dr. Silver, would you explain to the jury what psychomotor retardation is?

ME: Certainly. It's a psychologically noteworthy slowing of both movement and thinking, often associated with depression.

MR. HOSTILE: Now, when you said my client had signs of psychomotor retardation, this wasn't something that showed up on one of your psychological tests, was it?

ME: No, it was based on decades of experience...

MR. HOSTILE: Thank you Dr. Silver. You've answered my question.

ME: But...

MR. HOSTILE: I believe you've answered my question. Let me change focus a bit.

ME: OK.

MR. HOSTILE: I direct your attention back to behavioral observations that the jury may have taken note of right here in this courtroom: the jury's observation of your behavior.

Attorney Friendly: Objection, your honor! The witness is not a party to this lawsuit.

Judge Injustice: Objection overruled. You may proceed, Mr. Hostile.

MR. HOSTILE: When you were called to the witness stand, your hand appeared to be shaking. Was your hand shaking?

ME: Yes... but...

MR. HOSTILE: Thank you Dr. Silver. You've answered my question. And you looked unsteady on your feet. Are you feeling well?

ME: Quite well, thank you.

MR. HOSTILE: Dr. Silver, are you taking any medicine today?

ME: Yes.

MR. HOSTILE: Would you tell the jury the names of the medicines you've taken today?

ME: Amantadine, Ropinirole, Stalevo, Azilect...

MR. HOSTILE: That's sufficient, Dr. Silver. Those are four medicines that you've taken today prior to taking the witness stand?

ME: Yes.

MR. HOSTILE: Do any of those four medicines have known side effects?

ME: Virtually all medicines have side effects.

MR. HOSTILE: Including the four you've named?

ME: Yes. Including the four I've named.

MR. HOSTILE: Were you taking these same medicines when you conducted your IME with my client?

ME: Yes, I was.

MR. HOSTILE: I want to ask you about one of those medicines, Amantadine. Isn't Amantadine known to cause hallucinations in some people?

ME: That's correct.

MR. HOSTILE: And what is a hallucination, Dr. Silver?

ME: Well, basically, it's an idiosyncratic sensory experience—sights, sounds, scents that are not confirmed by the experience of others...

MR. HOSTILE: So, if I were to have a vision of some superhero standing next to you in this courtroom, might that be an example of a visual hallucination?

ME: Well, I guess it could be either a hallucination or Attorney Friendly to the rescue.

MR. HOSTILE: Doctor, let me repeat the question. We don't want you to guess. Would it be an example of a hallucination?

ME: Probably a hallucination.

MR. HOSTILE: And would it be correct to say that people who hallucinate are out of touch with reality?

ME: Probably.

MR. HOSTILE: Probably? Is there any doubt about it?

ME: Not much.

MR. HOSTILE: Would that be a "no," Doctor?

ME: It would.

MR. HOSTILE: So, Dr. Silver, you are here today giving sworn testimony regarding my client while you are taking medicine known to cause people to see, hear, and smell things that are not really there. Is that correct?

ME: Some, but not all, people have that reaction to the medicine.

MR. HOSTILE: How is the jury supposed to know if you're one of the people affected in that way? Never mind. Withdraw the question. I'd like to return to the matter of behavioral observations.

ME: OK.

MR. HOSTILE: We're in agreement that when you were called to the witness stand your hands may have been shaking?

ME: Yes, but...

MR. HOSTILE: Thank you doctor. And you were unsteady on your feet?

ME: I can explain that...

Mr. Friendly: Objection, your honor. Counsel is badgering the witness.

MR. HOSTILE: Judge, I request that the witness be instructed to answer the question.

Judge Injustice: Objection overruled. The witness is instructed to answer the question.

ME: I may have been unsteady on my feet.

MR. HOSTILE: Dr. Silver, in the course of conducting an IME, if you observed behavior like shaking hands and unsteadiness on one's feet, might you conclude that the person might be uncomfortable, anxious, apprehensive, not confident?

ME: If all I had to go on was the behavior observed, I might... but...

MR. HOSTILE: Pass the witness.

The work of an expert witness is tantamount to ritualized combat. I know my imagined adversary is only doing what he's obligated to do for the sake of his client. He may use whatever he can get away with to try to undermine my testimony. If he can't find a way to refute my opinion, he will try to counteract it by raising doubts about my mental soundness. I'm confident, however, that the next round would offer a relished opportunity to counter Hostile's assault on my credibility. I'd barely be able to contain my enthusiasm for the contest to come. This next round would be mine. Attorney Hostile would be mine.

But I just can't shake the feeling that it's not really fair to bring the potential additional baggage of my Parkinson's disease into the trial arena. It could hamper the side that sought my expertise, offering their opponent unmerited advantage before any evidence was even presented.

There is nevertheless a comforting aspect to forensic practice. That part of my work is very different from the world of psychotherapy. In a courtroom, I have no need to worry about protecting some hostile attorney's feelings. I have no intimate relationship with someone who is actively assaulting my credibility.

While I can do most forensic consulting from the comfort of my home study, there are specific circumstances (independent medical examinations, court appearances, and depositions) that may require travel. I'm capable of independent travel, but it becomes more difficult with age and progressing disease. Given air-travel unpredictability, I may not be at my physical and professional best by the time I arrive at my destination. I may well be incapable of immediate response to the crises and urgencies common to this work. A business trip from New Mexico to California underscored the dilemma.

Following two days of meetings in San Diego, I hurriedly taxi to the airport for a flight to Albuquerque and another daylong meeting the following morning. My connecting flight is delayed. It's near midnight when I reach my Albuquerque hotel, hours beyond my scheduled arrival time. For me, this is far more than a frustrating inconvenience. By that time of night, I'm well beyond my medication's effectiveness. It's difficult for me merely to move. Had I arrived just a few hours earlier, I might still have been expected to respond to some late-breaking issue. Rendering competent, coherent counsel from within a mobility-disordered body had clearly become an insurmountable challenge.

Prior to Parkinson's, I'd assumed that if my thinking remained sound, I would keep working through the remaining years. The disease is defeating my plan. Though fortunate that my ability to think clearly is still sound, my physical symptoms do present barriers to continued practice. When my psychotherapy patients became concerned about my increasingly obvious hand tremor, it seemed time to limit my work. Even before my patients put their feelings into words, I could see alarm in their eyes. The vector of concern had suddenly reversed. Instead of me worrying about *them,* they had begun to worry about *me.* That's just not how it's supposed to be. There was no way I could shield the intimate container of psychotherapy practice from intrusion by my Parkinson's symptoms.

Parkinson's disease aside, I've always had a gnawing fear of not knowing when my professional time has passed. I've dreaded the thought of staying beyond the peak of my competence and not being the first to know when it's over. I've seen colleagues who continued beyond their time. As a matter of personal and professional pride, I'm determined not to be one of them.

As Parkinson's has sped up my professional end-game, Lou Gehrig, the famous New York Yankees baseball player, and his 1939 farewell speech come to mind. I'm no Gehrig, Parkinson's is not ALS, and I may not be, as Gehrig declared himself, "the luckiest man alive." Nevertheless, the 45-year career that took me far from my Bronx beginnings to places I could barely have imagined, and that has challenged and rewarded me beyond expectations, makes me lucky indeed. And now, a trio of logistical, tactical, and timing concerns make a good case for acting sooner rather than later to bring this long, rewarding run to a quiet conclusion. Though I wish I could stay forever, the season to bid farewell to my life's work has now arrived. It's now time for me to be movin' on.

Too Soon Taken³

A joint boxing lesson was the last I would ever see of Larry, my friend and comrade in arms. The day following that last training session, Dianne and I were off on a three-week vacation. Upon our return, Larry and I were to pick up where we'd left off. Yet eight days after our last contact, I received a stunning message:

> *Hi Bob, It is with a heavy heart that [I] write to tell you that Larry ... had [a] major stroke yesterday. ... He is not expected to survive. His family has asked for privacy as he comes home to hospice care. I know that you two were friends and I thought you would want to know. I am so sorry to be the bearer of such sad news. He was a wonderful man, loved by many.*
>
> *Be well, Donna*

Months earlier, my stepson, Brad, had passed on a TV news report on boxing training as remarkably helpful physical therapy for Parkinson's patients. I forwarded the information to Larry. He responded enthusiastically and quickly arranged for joint weekly training sessions. The very thought of shuffling senior citizens in boxing gloves made us laugh. This unlikely image seemed to amuse others as well. At the start of our first training session, David, our trainer, announced, "Before we go any further, we need to give each of you a ring name. Larry, you are now 'Larry the Doctor.' Bob, you'll be 'Bob the Butcher.' I may even take you around to some bars and earn some money staging exhibitions."

My friendship with Larry was not among his longest or strongest, nor was it one of his nearest or dearest. Nevertheless, it likely occupied a special place among the relationships of his life. Our shared histories (Jewish men of similar age, born in The Bronx, having had long careers in helping professions, now nascent writers) might easily have been the basis for the deeper friendship we were sidling up to. Some short months earlier, we had exchanged drafts of our memoirs, perhaps in an unlabeled effort to hasten this process.

But it was Parkinson's disease, our common adversary, that propelled a special connection. Involuntarily conscripted into this group, we were automatic allies. Our bond was forged with reciprocal efforts to support and encourage one another in refusing to submit to our relentless foe. "To hell with Parkinson's disease," were Larry's recurring words.

And now, he is suddenly gone. A massive hemorrhagic stroke has claimed my fellow warrior. Over a thousand miles from home, I am awash in grief and disbelief. He was five years younger. I had counted on our partnership in the Parkinson's Iliad that lay before us. Older and longer ago diagnosed, I assumed I would be first to go.

With macabre irony, I recall a recent conversation with Larry regarding our ultimate demise. Perhaps motivated by a wish to encourage, a friend of his had naïvely implied that having Parkinson's conveyed immunity to other diseases. "At least you know what you've got," this friend had said. Larry and I laughed about it, once again recalling an old saying among physicians, "Just because you have ticks doesn't mean you can't have fleas." In Larry's case, the saying was prophetic: Parkinson ticks were ultimately trumped by killer fleas in the form of a stroke. It instantly preempted any possibility of the quality of a life that he wished to live. Six days later, he was gone.

Dianne and I barely arrived back home in time to be present at the community's celebration of Larry's life. Attended by easily a thousand fellow mourners, it included a video of him reading the essay that is the final chapter in his memoir, *A Life Well Worn*. Many months earlier, Dianne and I had been in the standing-room-only audience for the original reading of that essay, "The Other Side." It had been the concluding piece for the evening and was greeted with sustained, enthusiastic applause. As Dianne and I slowly headed for the exit, Larry spotted us and made his way to us through the scrum of well-wishers. Drawing near, he confided that my having previously written about my Parkinson's battle had encouraged him to read his Parkinson's piece in public. He added, "I read this for you." His unanticipated declaration brought me close to tears. Larry had no way of knowing that I had ambivalently scheduled an attempt to follow *his* lead early the next morning with an effort to summit Taos Ski Valley's 13,161-foot elevation Wheeler Peak.

Deeply uncertain as to my ability to reach the Wheeler summit, I began the trek as planned the following day. Larry's words from the prior evening stayed with me, filling me with determination to do my best to reach this unlikely goal for someone with Parkinson's disease. I'll never know what he had intended in his words for me the night before. Nevertheless, I felt inspired by his example. If he had done it, perhaps I could too. But this was not a competition. Rather, it was the informed encouragement of one battle-tested brother for another. I did in fact reach the summit that day. Had Larry known of my plan, he would have been pulling for me, as I would have been pulling for him. My continued journey with Parkinson's will be lonelier and harder without him. He was taken far too soon.

3) An earlier version of this essay appeared in the Op-Ed pages of *The Taos News*, March 10, 2016, A7.

Quest for the Cure[4]

This guy is unbelievably full of himself. Give me a break! What am I doing here? I can't believe this is what he's presenting. Just what I was afraid of. Thanks a lot, Virginia!

Jim and Virginia had each telephoned to encourage me to attend a rare local presentation by a presumably famous practitioner of traditional Chinese medicine (TCM). These dear friends were convinced that this visitor from the East had something miraculous to offer in relief of Parkinson's disease.

Virginia had called twice. She is a widely acknowledged devotee of all things Eastern. Her invitation is emotionally complicated for me. The unbidden concern for my well-being truly touches me. My deep skepticism notwithstanding, given Virginia's thoughtfulness, I cannot refuse to hear this man out. Ambivalently, I agree to attend.

The next night's cold mountain-winter weather finds Dianne and me making our way through the steadily falling snow. We're bound for one of Taos's alternative-medicine clinics. Along with my odd cohort — the halt, the lame, and the infirm — we are like pilgrims to Lourdes, seeking the equivalent of holy waters to cure our disabling afflictions.

Doctor "Han" had come to share the "good news" of the curative powers of acupuncture with the people of Taos. He'd arrived from Shanghai, China, and Orlando/Winter Park, Florida — fresh from his self-trumpeted worldwide lecturing tour — eager to introduce those who are suffering the many incapacities and indignities of Parkinson's to the vast curative powers of acupuncture. I have every intention of keeping my mouth shut and listening to the lecture with an open mind.

What is that old saying about the best-laid plans?

There we sit, some two dozen of us: the afflicted and those who love and care for us, packed cheek to jowl in a haphazardly furnished reception area. We're surrounded by shelves overflowing with large glass jars apparently harboring all manner of exotic herbal remedies.

A mismatched, rag-tag collection of chairs must be continually supplemented and rearranged to accommodate the continuous trickle of arrivals. All chairs are pointed toward a desk at the front of the room on which is precariously perched a video monitor of such small size that it is itself a sight to behold.

As I scan the growing crowd, I recognize several friends, fellow members in my diagnostic group.

Are they any more optimistic than I? If so, I pity these poor, naïve souls. Don't get your hopes up. You'll be sorry.

Doctor Han, a jovial, outgoing, high-energy speaker with a Chinese accent opens the program with a half-hour introduction to the TCM "theory" underpinning acupuncture (yin-yang; chi-blood, etc.). The language and concepts all are quite strange to me. Nevertheless, I'm committed to hearing the man out.

The program proceeds with fully *two hours* of video clips. First come a series of near-breathless, enthusiastic archival Florida TV news reports of the medical miracles performed by the good doctor. Then there are multiple patient testimonials and anecdotes demonstrating Han's astounding cures of a virtually limitless range of medical conditions. Indeed, it seems that he claims to cure almost anything.

Doctor Han holds center stage. He's the focus and the content of the program, presenting video-taped cure of patient after patient, interviewed cinema verité style with the distinguished doctor now gonzo journalist. Patient interviews are punctuated with Han's own interspersed monosyllabic commentary, deftly articulated in a repetitive, self-congratulatory "Wow!"

Endless patient testimonials are intermingled with self-declarations of the good doctor's medical and physical prowess, his remarkable international reputation, photographic documentation of his qi gong expertise, and a certificate confirming his international "Who's Who" listing: a veritable legend in his own mind. What a guy! Right here, in tiny, isolated Taos. What a miracle!

I can't take much more of this. I'll bet Dianne is just waiting for me to shoot my mouth off as usual. Everybody else seems able to just sit and listen. Don't be insulting.

Finally, I can no longer contain myself. My skeptical instincts get the best of me. The question and comment that I had been stifling for hours breaks the obedient attention of the reverent assembly.

Given their collective scowl, does the alternative-medicine community think I'm some agent-provocateur of the Western medical establishment?

"Doctor Han," I begin, "Are you going to take questions?"

"Yes, of course," is his enthusiastic reply.

Then the monologue begins.

"With all due respect (disrespectful comments are always preceded by this disclaimer), this is an audience of vulnerable and impressionable people.

Anecdotes and testimonials can only get us so far. We'd all like a miracle, but my experience is that when something seems to be too good to be true, it generally is. I am a product of Western scientific thought, and I wonder if you can point us toward some research supporting the effectiveness of these treatments?"

Doctor Han appears surprised and puzzled. He responds with his declaration of his personal "85 percent success rate."

"No, that's not what I'm asking about. I'm interested in empirical data, randomized clinical trials, double-blind studies."

Doctor Han appears even more puzzled. Then his handlers step in with ostensible efforts to translate and communicate the substance of my query. Their impromptu mini-briefing of Doctor Han does not seem to be taking hold. He continues to look befuddled.

Finally, I volunteer yet another comment.

"I looked at a review of the research this morning. The conclusion was that the data are 'not convincing.'"

An argumentative counterpoint then emerges, first from the clinic's visibly uncomfortable owner and forcefully joined by a visiting acupuncturist. "Narrow, limited methodology," is their uniform indictment of Western scientific method. Those

with that mind-set are ostensibly unable to compre-
hend the truths of TCM. This knowledge, I'm lec-
tured, has been around for 5,000 years. Who the hell
am I to argue with ancient history?

The audience begins to stir. By ones and by twos,
assembled members gravitate toward the exit. The
meeting is adjourning.

Have I torpedoed the gathering?

Who knows what promise this ancient wisdom
of the East may hold? I had no way to tell from what
had been a presentation of hype and recruitment.
It fed my innate skepticism instead of my yearning.

Early the next morning I'm up to my eyeballs in
the data that had been summarily dismissed by Doctor Han's minions. Yes, there it is, leaping out at me
from the computer monitor: "Not convincing." That,
indeed, is the bottom-line conclusion of the peer-re-
viewed, meta-analysis of studies of the efficacy of
acupuncture in the treatment of Parkinson's disease.
I'd not simply imagined science's disappointing sum-
mary judgment of Doctor H's work. Lee, Shin, Kong,
and Ernst had said so in a scholarly journal (*Movement Disorders,* August 2008). One can look it up!

The mildly damning "not convincing" had followed from an analysis of 11 separate research
reports of randomized clinical-trial investigations,
the gold standard for medical research. But to my
puzzlement and surprise, as I dig into the data,

there seem to be at least some complicated, qualified, mildly positive outcomes in several of the 11 investigations. There may be something there, despite the authors' conclusion of "not convincing." Is the devil in the details? Now, I'm really in a quandary. I find myself at odds with both sides in this virtual debate. Han had shamelessly propagandized. Lee, et al., had been cavalierly dismissive.

The whole thing represents a dilemma for me and for my fellow sufferers. Though by Western standards the evidence may not yet (if ever) be there, this alternative-medicine approach may actually offer something of value. It's hard to know, especially given that Doctor Han's presentation was so much the stuff of indoctrination and persuasion, and therefore reflexively repulsive to skeptics like me.

Do we follow our hearts or our heads? We know for sure that as far as the part of our head that controls our body's movements is concerned, our heads are not really doing so well. Our heads are certainly suspect. Perhaps our hearts will do better. The potential downside would likely be yet another dashed hope, another broken heart. What is a Parkinson's patient to do? Perhaps, in the end, we suspend disbelief, follow our dreams, and give it a try.

---

4) An earlier version of this essay appeared in R.J. Silver, *Tributes & Tirades: Taos Life and American Politics*, Nighthawk Press, 2013, pp. 43-46.

One Fine Day

The entire excursion was an unfolding of surprises. Dianne and I had driven hundreds of miles to Southern California, seeking seaside relief from our Northern New Mexico mountain winter. Our car was loaded to its limit with tennis racquets, bicycles, and golf clubs we couldn't use back home. Completing our California "endless summer" fantasy of respite and recreation, we'd rented a small cottage a couple of blocks from the Pacific shore.

Shortly after our arrival, Dianne chanced upon information regarding guided tours at the nearby Louis Kahn–designed Salk Institute for Biological Studies. I knew of Kahn's iconic standing as an architect and was vaguely aware of our proximity to "The Salk," but I hadn't given any prior thought to seeing it. Architecture fans that we are, we immediately registered for a tour. We were in for further surprises.

On arrival at the Institute's La Jolla location, we were stunned at our first sight of its spectacularly situated buildings. Sited on a bluff looking out toward the Pacific Ocean, the structures were at once starkly imposing and strongly inviting. Although more than half a century has passed since the Salk Institute's original buildings were designed and erected, they exude an abiding timelessness.

But beyond the compelling architecture of the place, this Salk-Kahn collaboration is far more than a monument to a magnificent man. The architecture seemed calculated to further the Institute's founding vision, the very embodiment of a grand "build it and they will come" dream.

Suggesting organizational insight at its best, this facility is an inspired research crucible, intended to attract, engage, and nurture the planet's best and brightest minds, and to stimulate them to produce nothing less than discoveries of causes and cures for mankind's intractable diseases. It's as if Salk was intent on replicating on a grand scale what he had done in eradicating the scourge of polio. Assembled here were the ingredients needed to bring this bold dream to fruition.

Our initial glimpse of the primary buildings was from a slightly below-grade travertine-stone courtyard. Passing through the entry space and up several wide steps toward the Institute's central buildings, we were met by Salk's words, carved in the stone beneath our feet.

"Hope lies in dreams, in imagination and in the courage of those who dare to make dreams into reality." Here, indeed, was concrete expression of mankind's most lofty aspirations borne by the courage of those who dare to dream of yet-unknown possibilities.

A bit further along was a grand plaza established by the juxtaposition of two main multistory structures. The buildings' mirroring facades form the two closed sides of an inviting expanse. We couldn't keep our hands off the surfaces of the painstakingly fabricated concrete primary construction material that looked and felt like marble.

Once beyond the plaza's broad opening, our eyes followed a ribbon of water coursing through a channel carved in the stone floor, bisecting the open space and terminating at the plaza's far end. The changing Pacific Ocean is framed in a large gap between the buildings at the most distant point. Awestruck by this space, I imagined sunset soirees drawing Institute scientists into fertile impromptu collaborative interaction. The narrow stream flowing out toward the Pacific seems to underscore the Institute's dynamic interaction with the natural world, proclaiming this not some detached ivory-tower enterprise but rather a river of endless possibilities. In apt metaphor for the Institute's drive to illuminate the darkness of our limited knowledge, "light wells," integral to the massive buildings' design, bring daylight to otherwise dark below-grade lab and office spaces.

As if our very visit to this officially designated world "Cathedral of Culture" had not already been surprise enough, there was more. Waiting among a dozen other tourists in the bright sunshine and cool breeze of the Southern California early afternoon, we were introduced to our guide, Leah. An Institute scientist, ordinary in appearance, she was casually dressed in the long-sleeved knit shirt and black leggings currently in vogue. I smugly assumed that her talk would be a stock warm-up for the architecture tour or a pitch for donations. Attention now on her, Leah launched into an informed, confident, articulate description of the Institute's research mission and programs. Her words and tone conveyed her dedication to the work she had undertaken. I was captivated and moved by her passionate presentation and her presence. Her words instantly pierced my heart's protective shield, moved my world, and left me stunned and speechless.

"... radically revised brain science ... brain stem cells ... neuroplasticity ... no longer believe number of brain cells fixed at birth ..."

Prior to Leah's talk, I had no idea what they were researching at The Salk. "Biological studies" can cover a lot of territory, and polio had long since been defeated. As Leah described the major themes of the Institute's research program, it became clear that she and her colleagues were decidedly in the hunt for, among other things, the scientific basis for a cure for Parkinson's disease — my disease. I was deeply moved. This intelligent, eloquent stranger and her gifted colleagues were committing their ability and energy to curing what specifically ails me! I'd had some abstract intellectual notion of scientific research being conducted on Parkinson's disease, but this was different. I was face-to-face with a real person devoted to my cure.

Though I know that Leah could not have had me specifically in mind in her work, the whole thing felt deeply personal. She had no knowledge of me as an individual. Yet she and unnamed others in this extraordinary place were devoting themselves to discovering the cause and cure for my disease. I was flooded with feelings of gratitude at the mere thought that a capable cadre of total strangers was so invested in my well-being. It was as if a small army of personal avatars were fiercely fighting to rescue me. Their unbidden commitment to improve the lives of faceless strangers like me must surely rank among the most generous, noble, and admirable of human capacities.

It may not come to pass in my lifetime, but I left the Salk Institute buoyed with hope that in this place, a cure will be found, one fine day.

Epilogue

More than a dozen years have passed since I was diagnosed with Parkinson's disease. I was 64 years old. Though my writing about Parkinson's may now have ended, my journey with the disease has not.

From my current vantage point, the initial prediction of a grim existence twelve years out seems unlikely. Frustrating? Oh, yes. Inconvenient? Yes again. But grim? No way! Life may indeed be grim for some Parkinson's patients, but it's not grim for me. I'll do everything in my power to see that "grim" doesn't define my life. With passing time, my symptoms become more difficult to manage, but managed they are. The disease isn't perfectly controlled, but there's an old saying: "Don't allow the search for the perfect to become the enemy of the good." This, I take to heart.

In the preceding essays, I hoped to tell the story of my first decade with Parkinson's: the binds, grinds, disappointments, prescribed therapies, improvised strategies, serendipitous solutions, and the search for solace. It's hard to imagine the texture of life's next decade, the uncharted territory. I'm determined, however, that there will be a next decade. I'm equally determined that I will do my darnedest to defy expectations. For me, there is no alternative. For better or worse, it's in my nature neither to give in nor give up.

I hope that my story may encourage others to question their possibly grim prognoses, and to not allow themselves to become inadvertent collaborators in the destruction of their hopes and dreams. Indeed, there is an impressive body of social science that confirms the powerful impact that expected outcomes have on shaping eventual reality.

My neurologist predicts another acceptable fifteen years for me, and I'm betting with her. That would put me at almost age 90, an advanced station in any life, Parkinson's or not. I intend to play life's end game with resolve.

That said, noting my activities outside the boundaries of typical Parkinson's-constrained possibilities, friends sometimes ask, "How do you do it?" While I have some thoughts as to characteristics that have served me well in this struggle, I would not want others to conclude that my attributes must be theirs. I typically respond with rather unenlightening clichés:

"You play the hand you're dealt. That's just how I'm wired."

My retreat to the cover of relatively shallow responses is, in part, motivated by my concern that my fellow Parkinson's patients not wrongly conclude that I believe that they, too, are capable of anything and everything that I've managed to do. Nothing could be further from the truth. None can know the myriad details of individual circumstances, strengths, and weaknesses that confront others. Each person brings a unique constellation of situations, skills, and capacities to the fight. Each person is faced with the challenge of harnessing a particular set of assets in securing their best possible personal quality of life. My exhortation to my comrades is simply that they not prematurely or unnecessarily settle for any less of life than they might have. This is what I've wished for myself.

Perhaps in the years to come, I'll have a better answer to the question of how I do "it." For now, I will play the hand that I've been dealt and hope that others in my Parkinson's cohort also keep on keepin' on.

Acknowledgments

Even for one who loves words, none are sufficient to acknowledge the depth of gratitude to my community of friends, family, medical professionals, and comrades in arms who have aided me in writing *Keepin' On: Living Well with Parkinson's Disease.* Many have helped in my search for a full life and for adequate language to describe my efforts to live that life.

My gratitude begins with my wife, Dianne Frost, constructive critic-in-residence, exercise coach, virtual personal trainer, informal editor, fact checker, supplemental memory, omnipresent caregiver. She has been with me almost every step of the way. "We're in this together," she said in the beginning. She has been true to her word. I also thank her for her tolerance of my sharing details of our private life that may be beyond her comfort level.

Talented writer, gifted teacher, scrupulous editor, advocate, and steadfast friend, Bonnie Lee Black has long labored to help me write more clearly, succinctly, and creatively to imagined readers. My shortcomings in this regard are not for her lack of much appreciated effort.

Steve Fox was my first writing instructor. His class at the University of New Mexico-Taos started me down a different writing path than I had known. He is a continuing source of constructive criticism, wise counsel, energetic encouragement, and treasured friendship. His editing ability contributed far more than mere technical skill to the writing in progress. Though dual relationships can often be dicey, the fact that Steve is both my friend and my editor resulted in an effort well beyond the confines of rigid roles.

Barbara Scott's "Final Eyes" scoured the manuscript in search of undetected final corrections. She did this with empathy, humor, grace and integrity, never allowing friendship to compromise her duty to root out words that did not work.

Rebecca Lenzini's wise and generous counsel was of enormous help in charting the manuscript's course through the thicket of the contemporary publishing world. Her Nighthawk Press is a treasured jewel within the Taos writers' community.

My many talented Taos and Santa Fe writing workshop colleagues have offered insightful comment and criticism on the work in progress: Margaret Hansen, Pat Pollard, E.J. Cunningham, Lucy Herrman, Eileen Kalinowski Wiard, Melissa Glarner, John Abeln, Sallie Bingham, Michael Burney, Donna LeFurgey, and Elaine Sutton (deceased) have been especially generous with thoughtful suggestions and ongoing encouragement.

Dirk Herrman and Don Keefe were actively supportive of my effort to cope with Parkinson's disease while simultaneously writing about it. Always curious and ever interested in the substance of my journey and the content of my writing, they have been immeasurably encouraging.

Charlotte Keefe and David Perez shared their theater expertise, helping me breathe life into the public reading of my words.

Harry Bransom graciously lent his considerable legal background to confirm the plausibility of an imagined courtroom exchange central to one of the chapters.

Jill Marjama-Lyons, M.D., expertly treats my movement disorder; Lucas Schreiber, M.D., treats all my other medical maladies; and Sidney Bender, M.D., retired neurologist and dear friend, keeps unbidden, though much appreciated, watch over me.

I would be unpardonably remiss if I failed to express my deep gratitude to my friends and acquaintances who populate the book's scenes and who continually enrich my life. Though they haven't explicitly consented to their roles becoming public, I could not have told my story without their presence. I hope they will understand and forgive any untoward presumption on my part.

Finally, I give thanks for my friends Lindsey Enderby and Johnny Morton, as well as for the memory of Larry Schreiber. They inspire me to keep on keepin' on.

About the Author

Psychologist by background and training, story-teller by nature, Parkinson's patient by chance, Robert Silver grew up in a gritty part of New York City, which probably predisposed him not to give in or give up. From the Bronx High School of Science (1960) to the City College of New York (B.A., 1965, Psychology), and to Indiana University (Ph.D., 1972, Psychology), his educational path carried him far from his Bronx beginnings.

Retired after 45 years of clinical and forensic-psychology practice, consulting, and university teaching, he is now immersed in writing. Taos, New Mexico—a small, isolated, mountain town—is home for him and his wife, abstract painter Dianne Frost. Silver's creative nonfiction has been published in *Chokecherries, Howl, Storied Recipes, and Storied Wheels* — Taos-inspired anthologies that express the quirky creativity of this magical place that some call "the soul of the Southwest." *Tributes & Tirades:*

Taos Life and American Politics (Nighthawk Press, 2013) is a collection of Silver's social and political commentaries.